CLIMATE IMPACT
GLOBAL WARMING SOLUTIONS

BY

ROBERT QUIGLEY & SELINA SHILPEE

Quigley Publications.

www.robertquigleyforpresident.com

Table of Contents

Chapter 1 4

Introduction 4

Chapter 2 20

Historical context 20

Chapter 3 28

Causes of Global Warming 28

Chapter 4 38

Impacts of Global Warming 38

Chapter 5 57

Mitigating Climate Change 57

Chapter 6 74

Climate Policies and Regulations 74

Chapter 7 91

Adapting to Climate Change 91

Chapter 8 106

Effective Actions Should Take......................................106

Chapter 9 117

Solutions to Global Warming.......................................117

Chapter 10 130

Hindrance to Global Warming Solutions 130

Chapter 12 153

Real-world Insights into Climate Change Solutions 153

Chapter 12 170

Conclusion..170

References 179

Chapter 1

Introduction

"We're not doing well in the fight against climate change. But we can still win if we act quickly." - Greta Thunberg, Climate Activist.

"If a country ruins its land, it ruins itself too. Forests are like the lungs of the earth. They clean the air and make us feel energized." Franklin D. Roosevelt, 32nd President of the United States.

"We're capable of accomplishing this. This is the largest social movement that has ever happened. We are capable of doing this. If people think we don't have the desire to make changes, they should remember that the desire to make changes can always be renewed."- Al Gore, former US Vice President and Chairman of the Climate Reality Project.

The ocean levels are increasing, cloud forests are vanishing, glaciers are liquefying, and fauna is striving to adapt. It is evident that human activity has contributed significantly to the warming of the planet over the last hundred years, as we continue to rely on modern technologies to fuel our daily lives. These gases, referred to as greenhouse gases, have surpassed levels that have not been observed in the past 800,000 years.

Although there are different effects on Earth's climate in various locations, we commonly use the term global warming to describe the overall outcome. Although some people may use the terms interchangeably, scientists use the term "climate change" to describe the complex and unpredictable shifts presently affecting our planet's climate and environmental systems. This is because certain regions experience temporary cooling, which does not indicate a warming trend.

Climate change encompasses an array of consequences such as extreme weather occurrences, alterations in wildlife distribution and habitats, escalation in ocean levels, and other related impacts. By releasing gases that trap heat in the atmosphere, humans are causing changes in the climate's natural cycles that sustain every living organism's survival.

How can we effectively stop human-induced warming and cope with the alterations that have already occurred. The future state of our planet with its coastlines, forests, farms, and snow-covered peaks is precarious as we endeavor to find solutions.

Definition of Global Warming

The phrase "global warming" pertains to the extended increase in Earth's atmospheric temperature due to human activities such as the combustion of fossil fuels, deforestation, and production, resulting in the emission of greenhouse gases (GHGs). Due to the trapping of heat in the atmosphere by GHGs, the weather patterns shift gradually and cause a rise in the temperature of the Earth.

Although "global warming" and "climate change" are often used synonymously, they actually denote separate phenomena. Climate change refers to alterations that occur over time in the Earth's temperature, humidity, air pressure, wind, precipitation patterns, and cloud behavior. The phrase "global warming" precisely pertains to the influence of greenhouse gases on the Earth's mean surface temperature and constitutes a contributing factor to climate alteration. Rising temperatures attributed to the presence of greenhouse gases can be referred to as global warming. In instances where discussing enduring alterations in the earth's atmospheric conditions, it is preferable to utilize the term "climate change."

The phrase "global warming" was first introduced by geochemist Wallace Broecker in his 1975 publication titled "Climatic Change: Are We Nearing a Known Event of Global Warming. " Despite this, as far back as 1820, scientists had already begun studying the impact of greenhouse gases on the climate of the Earth over a century earlier. The initial identification that the atmosphere of Earth aids in retaining the heat of the sun was observed by Joseph Fourier, a French researcher. The climate can be affected over extended periods by changes in the tilt and precession of the Earth's axis, as well as natural variations in its orbit, as noted by the Serbian astrophysicist Milutin Milankovitch. Over the years, experts and decision-makers have collaborated to enhance their understanding of atmospheric functioning and devise effective solutions to address the adverse impacts of climate change (GLOBAL WARMING, 2018).

Climate Change vs Global Warming

"Even though both "global warming" and "climate change" are commonly interchanged, they represent two separate concepts. " Conversely, climate change encompasses the wider alterations in the Earth's climate system, including shifts in temperature, precipitation trends, and the frequency and severity of extreme weather occurrences.

The fundamental reason behind global warming is the buildup of greenhouse gases, particularly carbon dioxide, in the atmosphere. The heat-trapping nature of these gases leads to a rise in the Earth's temperature caused by the sun. The release of greenhouse gases into the atmosphere is predominantly caused by agriculture, deforestation, and the utilization of fossil fuels for energy generation. Climate change is causing an increase in sea levels and the melting of glaciers and ice caps, leading to more severe and frequent natural disasters.

Conversely, the term "climate change" encompasses numerous alterations within Earth's climate system in a more overarching sense. These advancements can be triggered both by natural circumstances such as alterations in the Earth's orbit or volcanic eruptions, in addition to human actions. Climate change has the potential to modify not only temperature and weather patterns, but also sea levels, ocean currents, and the frequency and intensity of storms.

The concepts of climate change and global warming are linked, but they are not interchangeable. A perilous shift in the atmosphere refers specifically to the rise in temperature, while global warming pertains to the broader alterations in the environmental system. To communicate precisely about the reasons and consequences of a phenomenon, it is crucial to distinguish between these concepts.

In summary, while "global warming" and "climate change" carry distinct meanings, they are often employed interchangeably. Climate change encompasses the wider modifications in the Earth's climate system, whereas global warming pertains specifically to the rise in surface temperature due to greenhouse gas discharges. In order to engage in a productive discourse regarding these matters, it is crucial to employ the appropriate terminology with accuracy.

The Science Behind Global Warming

The rise of Earth's overall surface temperature attributed mainly to the accumulation of greenhouse gases, such as carbon dioxide, in the atmosphere is referred to as global warming. The science supporting the idea of global warming is based on extensive research conducted by scientists worldwide over the course of several decades utilizing various methods to study the Earth's climate changes throughout history.

The greenhouse effect is the foremost mechanism accountable for the rise in global temperatures. This phenomenon takes place when atmospheric gases such as carbon dioxide, methane, and water vapor ensnare the heat radiated from the Earth's surface. If it weren't for the greenhouse effect, the Earth's average temperature would be exceedingly low at -18°C, a temperature unsuitable for the survival of the majority of living organisms. As the level of greenhouse gases in the atmosphere increases, the greenhouse effect intensifies, leading to a rise in the Earth's average temperature.

The primary cause behind the rise of greenhouse gases in the atmosphere can be attributed to the utilization of finite energy resources, such as coal, oil, and natural gas, that release carbon dioxide into the environment. The buildup of greenhouse gases in the atmosphere can be attributed to various human activities such as agriculture and deforestation.

Scientists have employed a diverse range of methods to examine the transformation of Earth's climate throughout history. One of the most significant techniques is the utilization of ice cores that are formed in polar areas over several millennia. By examining the gases preserved in ice, scientists can decipher the historical climate conditions, including temperature and greenhouse gas levels in the atmosphere.

Two additional techniques employed in the examination of global warming are the study of tree rings for insights into historical precipitation and temperature trends, as well as the utilization of satellite data to track changes in surface temperature and glacial coverage.

The agreed upon viewpoint among scientists is that the Earth's temperature is increasing and that human actions are the main cause. The IPCC, which is made up of scientists from various countries, has determined that the Earth's surface temperature has climbed by roughly 1°C since the pre-industrial era, with human actions likely being responsible for most of the warming that has taken place since the mid-20th century.

The effects of global warming are substantial and have wide-ranging implications. There are several consequences to consider, such as decreased biodiversity and ecosystem services, along with an increase in sea levels and extreme weather phenomena such as heatwaves, droughts, and storms. The influences of these consequences have far-reaching effects on various aspects such as transportation, agriculture, public health, and national security, leading to notable economic, social, and environmental outcomes.

Years of extensive research done by numerous scientists worldwide have substantiated the scientific principles underlying the phenomenon of global warming. The primary factor contributing to global warming is the buildup of greenhouse gases in the atmosphere, which is predominantly caused by the combustion of fossil fuels. The consequences of climate change are noteworthy and pressing, demanding swift action to reduce the discharge of greenhouse gases and adapt to the existing impact.

Importance of Discovering Solutions to Global Warming

The rise in the Earth's temperature is due to the accumulation of greenhouse gases in the atmosphere, creating a heat-trapping effect. The increase in temperature is having adverse effects on the environment in several ways. Several outcomes that could result from climate change are increased occurrences and severity of natural disasters, higher ocean levels, as well as changes in weather patterns that may impact both sustenance supplies and public health.

Acknowledging the importance of discovering remedies for global warming is crucial. Reducing the amount of greenhouse gases released is crucial in putting a stop to the progression of climate change. Lowering energy usage, adopting sustainable energy sources, and enhancing energy efficiency in transportation and constructions are some of the methods to achieve this.

Replenishing forests and utilizing carbon capture and storage techniques are vital strategies and technologies that aid in decreasing greenhouse gas levels in the atmosphere while also minimizing emissions. These remedies could aid in reducing the impacts of past air pollution and steering the world toward a more sustainable path.

The battle against climate change not only poses challenges but also offers prospects for economic growth, particularly through the innovation of new technologies and the reinforcement of the renewable energy industry. Moreover, tackling climate change can enhance public health by reducing respiratory illnesses through the reduction of air pollution.

The impacts of global warming are vast and comprehensive on every facet of human existence. The ascent of sea levels due to the thawing of glaciers and ice caps is jeopardizing low-lying regions and nations surrounded by water bodies. Natural disasters such as hurricanes, floods, and droughts are becoming more severe and frequent, causing both economic damages and forcing people to migrate.

Discovering remedies for global warming is crucial as they can assist in lessening its impacts and averting the most severe outcomes. Despite this, addressing the issue of climate change involves more than just decreasing emissions and investing in new technologies. Examples of this include advocating for the use of public transport, reducing meat consumption, and endorsing policies that promote renewable energy sources and increased energy efficiency.

The importance of finding solutions to global warming extends beyond national boundaries. The phenomenon of climate change is a matter of worldwide concern that calls for collaborative efforts among nations. Collaboration on a global level, together with accords such as the Paris Agreement, is essential in tackling the issue of climate change with success.

Discovering remedies for the predicament of global warming is an urgent matter. Postponing action on climate change will make it more challenging for us to prevent the severe consequences. It is imperative that we take prompt and decisive action in tackling environmental change and building a viable future. Promoting sustainability and minimizing emissions demands the joint efforts of individuals and communities to endorse policies and practices in favor of these goals. By collaborating with each other, we can discover resolutions to combat global warming and construct a superior future for both present and forthcoming generations.

The Urgency of Climate Change

It is imperative that we take prompt action to lessen the impacts of climate change, which is currently one of the most pressing obstacles we face. The agreement among scientists is that the cause of climate change can be attributed to human activities. The IPCC has cautioned that the planet's temperature is expected to increase by 1. 5 degrees Celsius in the next 20 years compared to pre-industrial levels, signaling catastrophic outcomes for the environment and its dwellers.

Due to the critical danger climate change poses to both the survival of human civilization and the ecosystems of the planet in the long run, urgent measures must be implemented to address it. Due to climate change, the elevation of sea levels will increase, leading to the displacement of countless coastal inhabitants. Moreover, it is causing a rise in the occurrence and intensity of environmental calamities such as prolonged dry spells, inundations, and cyclones, all of which pose risks to people's well-being and income.

Climate change is having an impact on agriculture, food security, and water resources. Changes in temperature and precipitation patterns are currently affecting crop productivity and water supplies, and this will have future implications for the accessibility and affordability of food and clean drinking water.

The urgency to combat the impacts of climate change intensifies with the realization that it will become more challenging and expensive to address if we delay taking action. The IPCC has issued a warning that reducing greenhouse gas emissions by 45% until 2030 and reaching a state of net-zero emissions by 2050 is necessary to limit global warming to 1. 5°C Achieving this goal will require changes in both consumer habits and governmental policies, alongside substantial investments in innovative technologies such as renewable energy, carbon capture and storage, among others.

The pressing nature of climate change is not only a matter of science but also of morality. Those who reside in developing nations, indigenous populations, and low-income areas are particularly susceptible to the impacts of climate change. Although they are the least responsible for greenhouse gas emissions, these communities are the ones most at risk from the impacts of climate change.

To better comprehend the pressing matter of climate change, it's crucial to scrutinize the existing global impacts that are already evident. In recent years, communities and ecosystems in Australia and California have been devastated by wildfires, causing massive financial losses and posing severe health hazards caused by smoke and air contamination.

The impacts of climate change extend beyond just wildfires, as extreme weather phenomena such as heatwaves, hurricanes, and floods are also being exacerbated. The far-reaching effects of these occurrences encompass various domains, including transportation, agriculture, public health, and national security, and have noteworthy impacts on economic, social, and environmental aspects. According to a Nature publication, global economic output may encounter a decline of up to 25% by the end of the century if the matter of climate change remains unaddressed.

As temperatures rise and weather patterns change, ecosystems are suffering from greater levels of degradation and fragmentation. This has a detrimental impact on various areas, ranging from food security to public health.

The Earth's climate system is nearing critical points, underscoring the pressing need to address climate change. A point of no return is reached when a system surpasses a threshold and enters a new phase that may be irreversible. If we persist in releasing greenhouse gases in the same quantity, then it is probable that we will initiate the melting of Greenland's ice sheet.

It is vital to acknowledge that addressing climate change encompasses more than just reducing the release of greenhouse gases. It includes building up toughness and reacting to the effects that already exist. One way to tackle the impact of climate change is to invest in resilient infrastructure, devise innovative strategies for conserving energy and water, and safeguard people who are at greater risk.

The importance of addressing environmental change cannot be overstated. An intricate and baffling concern that poses significant threats to the sustainability of human advancement and the ecosystems of the planet. The longer we delay taking action, the more challenging and expensive it will be to tackle its consequences. By collaborating to reduce greenhouse gas emissions, invest in clean energy, and address the consequences of climate change, we can build a more durable and eco-friendly future for ourselves and those to come.

Why Action is Necessary Now

Due to the current and projected exacerbation of global warming's consequences worldwide, immediate action towards addressing climate change is imperative. The Earth's surface temperature has risen approximately 1 degree Celsius since the pre-industrial era, resulting in several unfavorable repercussions for both the environment and humanity.

One of the most urgent consequences of global warming is the escalation in the severity and occurrence of natural calamities such as hurricanes, floods, and wildfires. The economy is incurring losses due to the migration of individuals resulting from these occurrences. The increasing ocean levels pose a threat to the existence of areas with low elevation and countries consisting of islands.

Food production is being impacted and species are either moving away or facing extinction due to shifts in weather conditions. Immediate action is necessary to prevent the escalation and expansion of the negative impact. As per the Intergovernmental Panel on Climate Change (IPCC), the planet could witness catastrophic consequences if the global warming level spikes to 1. 5 degrees Celsius by 2030. The IPCC issued this caution.

Postponing efforts to address climate change will exacerbate the difficulties and expenses of tackling it later on. If we delay, we will increasingly depend on technologies that may not even be developed yet and have to adjust to the unavoidably forthcoming impacts of climate change.

By taking action on climate change at present, the opportunity arises to construct a society that is both more durable and eco-friendly. By shifting towards sources of energy that are renewable, improving energy efficiency, and investing in eco-friendly infrastructure, opportunities for employment can be generated while simultaneously lowering air pollution levels and enhancing public health. Moreover, it could aid us in reducing the most adverse outcomes of climate change and protecting the Earth for upcoming cohorts.

Since the impacts of climate change are already noticeable, urgent measures to tackle it need to be taken. Postponing measures will merely increase the complexity and expenses involved in resolving the matter later on. By taking action now, it is within our reach to avert the most severe consequences of climate change, construct a more durable and eco-friendly society, safeguard the planet for tomorrow's populace, and adapt accordingly.

In addition to the impacts of climate change, several other justifications exist for taking prompt action. One key reason why collective action from all nations is necessary is due to the global nature of climate change. In order to adequately confront the issue of climate change, it is imperative for nations to collaborate and establish pacts such as the Paris Agreement.

Nowadays, taking action on climate change is crucial due to the fact that it is related to the fundamental rights of individuals. Climate change disproportionately affects disadvantaged communities, including those with limited financial resources, minorities, and indigenous groups. Because they often lack resources, these communities bear the smallest burden of responsibility for climate change. It's crucial to take action on climate change to ensure marginalized communities are able to adapt and not be left behind.

Moreover, engaging in efforts towards addressing environmental issues can also yield economic benefits. The transition towards a low-carbon economy presents promising opportunities for job creation and stimulation of growth. By putting money into renewable energy technologies like wind turbines and solar panels, businesses can benefit from reduced costs and greater energy stability, as these alternatives are becoming more cost-effective compared to traditional fossil fuels.

To ensure the preservation of life on Earth, it is imperative that we tackle the issue of climate change and its impact on biodiversity and ecosystems. Climate change-induced migration or extinction of species could bring about a domino effect on entire ecosystems. To ensure the sustainability of the Earth for the forthcoming generations, it is vital to conserve the variety of life and safeguard the surroundings.

Several variables require prompt action concerning the issue of climate change. Taking action on climate change can not only safeguard the biodiversity and ecosystems on our planet but can also provide economic benefits. By taking action in the present, we have the power to create a future that is both fair and ecologically sustainable for all.

Why This Book

Life as we understand it faces a significant threat as a result of an unparalleled environmental disaster that the world is presently encountering. The severity of global warming is escalating due to heightened temperatures, more frequent natural disasters, and considerable ecological damage. The critical state of affairs demands prompt action to prevent any further damage.

Fortunately, there are viable solutions to address this matter, which implies that it can be resolved. This publication provides a comprehensive analysis of the most effective approaches to addressing climate change, utilizing the latest scientific discoveries and technological breakthroughs. We firmly believe that if we unite and make firm and impactful decisions, we can establish a sustainable tomorrow that benefits not only the present but also future generations.

Each year, the effects of global warming become more evident as temperatures rise, natural disasters occur more frequently, and ecosystems suffer extensive damage.

The aim of this piece is to provide a comprehensive summary of the current state of climate change and its impact on the surroundings. Our focus will be on exploring the scientific foundation for global warming and its effects on various ecosystems and human societies. In addition, we will examine the impacts of climate change on politics and finances, and explore the strategies employed to address this pressing issue.

The primary aim of this book is to offer practical solutions to the issues that arise as a result of climate change. Thorough examination will be carried out on the most effective strategies to reduce greenhouse gas emissions, prepare for the impacts of climate change and promote sustainable development. Our goal is to present a compelling case for urgent measures to combat climate change by incorporating the latest research and data.
The pressing nature of the issue coupled with the scarcity of easily accessible details about viable remedies make it imperative to release a book that tackles potential resolutions for

the problem of climate change. Despite the abundance of scientific proof, there is a considerable discrepancy between awareness and implementation when it comes to addressing the detrimental consequences of climate change. Many individuals are cognizant of the problem at hand yet lack knowledge about how they can aid, while others remain uncertain about the gravity of the circumstances.

This book strives to address the gap by offering easily accessible, precise, and current data on the best strategies to alleviate the impacts of climate change. Our goal is to motivate people to take action promptly by presenting a thorough analysis of the issue, including its origins and consequences. We will be discussing cutting-edge scientific discoveries, policy alterations, and innovative technologies that can aid in resolving this issue.

This book aims to educate policymakers, researchers, and the public on the most effective methods for addressing the issue of climate change. Additionally, it will offer a platform for professionals and individuals with vested interests from diverse areas to engage in dialogue and cooperate towards establishing a viable future, instigating a conversation on the ways we can cooperate to achieve sustainability.

This book is indispensable as it provides pragmatic answers to the most urgent environmental problem of our era, along with vital insights related to it. Our expectation is that it will encourage people to take action, spark their creative ideas, and aid in the development of a planet that can uphold its own sustainability for years to come.

Chapter 2

Historical context

Industrialization and Global Warming

Before the onset of industrialization on our planet, the climate remained relatively constant. At this juncture, the climate on Earth was mainly influenced by natural factors such as solar activity, volcanic eruptions, and the Earth's rotation around the sun. The Earth's climate remained stable due to the natural mechanisms of the carbon and water cycles, which kept the climate system in balance.

From the late 1700s onwards, the start of industrialization sparked a noticeable shift in the Earth's climate due to human actions. Fossil fuels such as coal, oil, and natural gas emit significant amounts of carbon dioxide into the atmosphere. The increase in carbon dioxide concentrations has caused a rise in global temperatures, leading to alterations in the ecological system.
The noteworthy consequence of industrialization on the climate is the increase in severe weather occurrences.

Instances of hurricanes, heat waves, droughts, and floods are on the rise, and they are getting more intense, causing notable harm to buildings and essential facilities while also endangering the well-being and safety of human beings. The process of industrialization has also played a role in the depletion of forests, resulting in an augmented level of carbon dioxide in the atmosphere.

The impact of industrialization on climate has worsened due to the progression of technology. Although technology has brought about substantial advancements in society, it has also led to a rise in the release of harmful greenhouse gases. An increase in the usage of fossil fuels due to the adoption of transportation technology has resulted in a rise in carbon dioxide levels in the atmosphere.

Despite the considerable influence of technology and industrialization on climate change, endeavors are underway to mitigate the consequences of the phenomenon. The emergence of eco-friendly energy sources such as hydropower, wind power, and solar power exhibits promising potential in reducing the emission of greenhouse gases to a considerable extent. Furthermore, endeavors are undertaken to diminish the amount of refuse produced and augment the effectiveness of energy usage within industrial operations. (Masson-Delmotte et al., 2018).

The climate of the Earth has been significantly altered as a result of industrialization and technological advancements. The expansion in ozone-harming substance discharges has prompted a climb in worldwide temperatures, bringing about additional continuous and serious outrageous climate occasions and dangers to human well-being and security. Nonetheless, there are additional endeavors in progress to relieve the impacts of unnatural weather change, including the advancement of sustainable power sources and enhancements in energy proficiency.

Climate Before 1815 When Industrialization did not Hit the Earth

Climate change has piqued people's interest for many years. Climate change can be dated back to centuries ago when humans had negligible impact on the environment. Before 1815, the climate was fairly constant and fluctuations or variations were not noticeably apparent. The climate of the Earth was significantly influenced by natural occurrences such as solar activity, changes in the Earth's orbit, and volcanic outbursts.

The climate was significantly influenced by volcanic eruptions prior to the rise of industrialization. The emission of huge amounts of sulfur dioxide from volcanoes resulted in the formation of sulfuric acid particles that significantly reduced the amount of sunlight reaching the surface of the Earth. The outcome manifested in the form of winters characterized by volcanic activity, which had a cooling impact on the planet's weather patterns. The cooling effect caused by the eruption of Mount Tambora in 1815 led to crop failure and famine in various parts of the world. (STOTHERS, 1984).

Prior to the industrial era, solar activity was yet another natural element that influenced the climate. The amount of solar radiation reaching the Earth's surface is impacted by the sun's energy output variations over time. The fluctuation in solar activity, particularly during periods of low solar activity known as solar minimums, has been associated with climate changes. The period known as the Maunder Minimum, which occurred in Europe from 1645 to 1715, coincided with a decline in temperature. (EDDY, 1976).

The Earth's orbit and tilt had a substantial impact on climate change before the advent of industrialization. The Earth's path around the sun is not a flawless circle, but instead, it takes the form of an elliptical shape, varying in the level of eccentricity. Climate variations are brought about by the changes in Earth's orbit which lead to differences in the degree of solar radiation that reaches its surface. Moreover, the Earth's inclination plays a significant role in determining the seasons as it fluctuates, impacting the distribution of solar energy across the globe. These elements may have played a role in previous variations in climate, such as the occurrences of ice ages. The IMBRIE article of 1980 uses the term Milankovitch cycles to refer to this phenomenon as a whole. (IMBRIE, 1980).

Prior to the advent of industrialization, there were other factors that played a role in shaping the climate, besides the ones that are typically cited as being natural. Forests and other natural habitats played a significant role in regulating the Earth's climate, thus making them essential. Forests act as carbon sinks by absorbing carbon dioxide from the atmosphere and thus, play a pivotal role in reducing the greenhouse effect. Forests play a significant role in maintaining a balanced water cycle as they facilitate rainfall and prevent the erosion of soil. The creation of significant natural habitats also resulted in the development of microclimates that facilitated the flourishing of diverse types of flora and fauna.

The climate was influenced by geological transformations like the creation of mountains and plate tectonics which occurred gradually over time, before the era of industrialization. The geological shifts had an impact on both ocean currents and atmospheric circulation, which ultimately had an effect on the climate patterns. As an example, the formation of the Indian Monsoon system, which plays a key role in the weather patterns of South Asia, can be attributed to the presence of the Himalayan Mountain.

Before the onset of industrialization, the impact of human actions on climate change was relatively insignificant, and this is a crucial point to bear in mind. The temperature was affected by changes in land's albedo caused by deforestation and agriculture. Although humans also created methane and carbon dioxide as greenhouse gases, the amounts were considerably lower than what was produced in the industrial era.

Climate change was caused by natural factors like solar activity, variations in Earth's orbit and tilt, the presence of natural habitats, and changes in geology prior to industrialization. Climate change was also caused by human activities, though at much lower levels than during the industrial era. For understanding the current climate and predicting changes in the future, it is essential to comprehend the past climate and the factors that influenced it.

How Industrialization Impacts Global Warming in 100-200 Years

It is expected that the repercussions of industrialization on climate change will persist for a substantial period of time, possibly spanning over the next 100 to 200 years. The utilization of machinery and technology to manufacture goods on a massive scale constitutes the process of industrialization. Since the 18th century, it has initiated in Europe and North America and now has a global presence, as indicated by Boudreaux (2020). The leading catalyst for industrialization is the combustion of fossil fuels for energy and transportation, which produces considerable atmospheric emissions of carbon dioxide (CO_2) and other greenhouse gases.

The levels of atmospheric CO_2 have increased significantly since the Industrial Revolution, going from 280 ppm to more than 400 ppm currently, as per NASA's latest report. The predominant cause of CO_2 escalation, as predicted in IPCC's 2018 report, is the prolonged and foreseeable combustion of fossil fuels.

Because CO_2 remains in the atmosphere for an extended period, it is expected that the impact of industrialization on climate change will persist for several centuries. The IPCC report from 2018 indicates that the presence of CO_2 in the atmosphere could result in continued warming of the earth for numerous centuries, regardless of the cessation of all emissions. Furthermore, the ongoing industrialization of developing countries is anticipated to cause an increase in worldwide greenhouse gas emissions during upcoming years, stated by the UNDP in 2021.

To combat the effects of industrialization on global warming, we need to transition to cleaner energy sources and reduce the release of greenhouse gases. As per the IPCC report of 2018, substantial changes to energy generation, transportation, and infrastructure, along with global collaboration and investment in innovative technologies will be imperative. Fortunately, there are various methods available to reduce emissions of ozone-depleting substances. These include utilizing eco-friendly energy sources such as wind, solar, and hydroelectric power, enhancing the energy efficiency of buildings and transportation, and implementing strategies to decrease emissions from industry and agriculture, according to the EPA in 2021.

The process of industrialization has notably played a major role in causing the increase in global temperatures during the last few centuries. Moreover, this trend is likely to persist for another century or even two. The fundamental cause of industrialization is the combustion of fossil fuels which leads to an upsurge in greenhouse gas emissions, specifically CO_2, that induce the confinement of heat and contribute to the phenomenon of global warming. The impact of industrialization on global warming requires major changes in energy production, transportation, infrastructure, international collaboration, and investment in innovative technologies.

Impact of Technological Advancements on Global Warming

The connection between technological advancements and global warming is the subject of ongoing debate. While technological advancements have the potential to lessen the impact of climate change and reduce emissions of greenhouse gases, they also have the potential to increase emissions and exacerbate the issue. In this section, we'll look at a few of the most important ways that technological advancements have affected global warming.

The production and consumption of energy has changed as a result of technological advancements, which is one of the primary ways in which they have affected global warming. By displacing energy sources based on fossil fuels, advancements in renewable energy technologies like solar and wind power have the potential to significantly reduce greenhouse gas emissions (IEA, 2021). Energy consumption and emissions can also be reduced through improvements in energy efficiency, such as more energy-efficient buildings and appliances.

Nevertheless, mechanical headways can likewise add to expanded outflows through the improvement of new ventures and items. Energy consumption and electronic waste, for instance, have significantly increased as a result of the technology industry's expansion and the rise in electronic device use (UNEP, 2019). In a similar vein, the expansion of the aviation industry has resulted in an increase in air travel-related emissions (ICCT, 2022).

Changes in agriculture and land use are another way that technological advancements have influenced global warming. Food production has increased as a result of advancements in agricultural technology, such as the use of fertilizers and irrigation (Bélanger & Pilling, 2019). However, these advancements have also contributed to deforestation, soil degradation, and an increase in agricultural emissions. Changes in land use, like urbanization and industrialization, can also make emissions go up and biodiversity goes away.

It is essential to take into account both the potential advantages and disadvantages of technological advancements when evaluating their impact on global warming. As we previously mentioned, the utilization of renewable energy technologies has the potential to significantly lessen emissions of greenhouse gases and lessen the effects of climate change. However, advancements in technology can also increase emissions and exacerbate the issue.

The transportation industry is one significant way that technological advancements have affected global warming. Emissions from the transportation sector have decreased as a result of the rising popularity of electric vehicles (EVs) (IEA, 2020). Additionally, future advancements in traffic management systems and the creation of autonomous vehicles have the potential to further reduce transportation-related emissions (McKinsey & Company, 2021). However, it is essential to keep in mind that the manufacturing and disposal of EV batteries may have an impact on the environment (UNEP, 2021).

The use of carbon capture and storage (CCS) technologies is another way that technological advancements have affected global warming. CCS technologies have the potential to reduce emissions by capturing and storing underground carbon dioxide emissions from industrial processes (IEA, 2021). However, high costs and regulatory obstacles have hampered the application of CCS technologies (Global CCS Institute, 2021).

Further, It is also important to note that individual behavior and consumption patterns can influence the impact of technological advancements on global warming. For instance, the use of video streaming services has skyrocketed in recent years, raising emissions from devices and data centers (IEA, 2020). Similarly, emissions from manufacturing and waste disposal have been impacted by the expansion of the fast fashion industry and increased consumer demand for disposable goods (MacArthur, 2017).

It is crucial to keep in mind that the social, economic, and political contexts in which technologies are developed and utilized are just as important as the technologies themselves in determining the impact of technological advancements on global warming. The availability of financing, political support, and regulatory frameworks, for instance, may limit the application of renewable energy technologies (IRENA, 2022).

In general, technological advancements have a complex and multifaceted effect on global warming. While some technologies have the potential to lessen the effects of climate change, others have the potential to raise emissions and make the situation worse. As we move towards a more practical future, it is critical to painstakingly think about the ecological effect of new advances and take a stab at a harmony among development and manageability.

Chapter 3

Causes of Global Warming

As we have previously discussed, human activity is responsible for the complex issue known as global warming. Global warming is chiefly caused by the emission of greenhouse gases such as carbon dioxide (CO2), methane (CH4), and nitrous oxide (N2O) into the atmosphere. In this chapter, we'll delve more deeply into the factors that contribute to global warming and their impact on the environment.

There is no denying that the actions of humans are a major factor in the occurrence of climate change. Therefore, it is imperative that we take action to decrease our carbon footprint and stop its advancement. For several decades, scientists have been studying the origins and ramifications of global warming, and their findings indicate that human actions are primarily responsible for this phenomenon, according to the IPCC's (2018) report.

Global warming arises from various factors, including deforestation, urbanization, burning fossil fuels, industrial practices, as well as agricultural and livestock techniques. In the upcoming chapter, we will explore these as well as other variables. We will further discuss the environmental impact of these activities and explore potential solutions for minimizing their effects.

It is imperative in our endeavors to address climate change that we gain a thorough understanding of the factors contributing to the phenomenon of planetary warming. By acknowledging the elements that contribute to the issue, we can devise successful remedies to diminish our carbon emissions and preserve the earth for generations to come.

Fossil Fuels and Their Impact on Climate Change

In a substantial manner, fossil fuels have powered the growth of modern industrialization and economic expansion. Nevertheless, the chief origin of greenhouse gas releases that add to the advancement of global warming is the burning of these resources. When fossil fuels are burned, they emit carbon dioxide (CO2) which gets released into the atmosphere, causing the planet to heat up by trapping heat.

According to the International Energy Agency (IEA) (2021), the energy sector is responsible for about 75% of the worldwide greenhouse gas emissions. Fossil fuels such as coal, oil, and gas are the key sources of energy for heating, transportation, and electricity production. Due to our persistent dependence on these sources of energy, there is a steady increase in atmospheric CO2 levels, leading to the exacerbation of the impacts of climate change.

Climate change, resulting from the usage of fossil fuels, is leading to a plethora of negative consequences such as the escalation in sea levels and the amplification of the intensity and recurrence of extreme weather conditions. The United Nations' IPCC has raised an alarm over the harmful effects of sustained fossil fuel usage, stating that a temperature surge of 1. 5 degrees Celsius above pre-industrial measures is inevitable and likely to have disastrous implications for the environment and humanity, as per their 2018 report.

To reduce the impact of fossil fuels on climate change, it is imperative to transition towards alternative, greener sources of energy such as hydroelectric, wind, and solar power. The utilization of electric cars and public transportation is an effective approach to reducing carbon emissions caused by transportation. Governments and corporations have the option to employ carbon capture and storage technology to grab emissions of carbon dioxide produced by the combustion of fossil fuels, which can subsequently be preserved in underground storage.

The utilization of fossil fuels is the main cause of climate change, and if we persist in using them, it could profoundly endanger both humanity and the environment. The imperative need of the hour is to adopt alternative energy sources and technologies that are sustainable and generate minimal greenhouse gas emissions, thereby moving away from traditional fossil fuels. The actions taken presently will determine the impact that climate change will have on future generations.

The Effects of Deforestation on The Environment

Deforestation is one of the huge reasons for an Earth-wide temperature boost, representing around 10% of worldwide ozone-harming substance outflows. Trees assimilate CO_2 from the air and convert it into oxygen through the course of photosynthesis. Nonetheless, when trees are chopped down or consumed, the carbon put away in them is delivered into the environment, adding to the expansion of ozone-depleting substances. Deforestation likewise disturbs the water cycle, prompting soil disintegration, diminished water quality, and loss of biodiversity. Besides, forestlands go about as carbon sinks, and that implies they store more carbon than they discharge.

The deficiency of woodlands brings about a decrease in carbon sinks, further adding to a dangerous atmospheric deviation. The expansion in worldwide temperatures likewise straightforwardly affects backwoods, as it prompts dry seasons, out-of-control fires, and other ecological perils that compromise their reality. Hence, it is pivotal to address deforestation and take on feasible forestland the executive's practices to relieve the impacts of a dangerous atmospheric deviation.

One illustration of supportable backwoods the executives rehearses is the REDD+ program, which represents Diminishing Outflows from Deforestation and Timberland Corruption. The program means to boost emerging nations to lessen deforestation by furnishing them with monetary assets and specialized help to help supportable land use rehearses (REDD+, 2021). Moreover, reforestation and afforestation endeavors can likewise help in moderating the effect of deforestation on the climate. These practices include establishing new timberlands and trees in regions where they have been recently eliminated or didn't exist.

Notwithstanding its effect on environmental change, deforestation additionally has critical biological outcomes. Woods are fundamental territories for some plant and creature species, and deforestation can prompt the deficiency of biodiversity and the annihilation of whole biological systems (FAO, 2021). Deforestation likewise adds to soil disintegration, as tree attaches help to secure soil set up and forestall disintegration (Milesi et al., 2005). Without these roots, soil can be handily washed away during weighty precipitation or amazed by wind, prompting diminished soil richness and expanded sedimentation in neighboring streams.

Moreover, deforestation can likewise prompt an expansion in the recurrence and seriousness of catastrophic events, like floods, avalanches, and fierce blazes (FAO, 2021). This is on the grounds that backwoods assume a significant part in controlling water cycles, retaining precipitation, and delivering it gradually after some time. Without trees to assimilate the water, precipitation can immediately run off the outer layer of the land, prompting streak floods and disintegration. Also, woodlands go about as regular firebreaks, and their expulsion can prompt more continuous and extremely fierce blazes.

Deforestation likewise fundamentally affects nearby environments, as it disturbs the sensitive harmony between species and assets. It prompts soil disintegration, loss of natural surroundings for some species, and expanded weakness to outrageous climate occasions like floods and avalanches. Deforestation additionally diminishes the capacity of woodlands to go about as carbon sinks and to direct neighborhood environments by influencing temperature, stickiness, and precipitation designs.

To resolve the issue of deforestation, it is essential to advance economical land use rehearses and to safeguard and reestablish timberlands. This can incorporate measures, for example, decreasing the interest for items that add to deforestation, implementing guidelines against unlawful logging and land use, and advancing reforestation and afforestation endeavors. By safeguarding and reestablishing backwoods, we can diminish ozone-harming substance discharges, safeguard biodiversity, and advance the well-being and prosperity of neighborhood networks.

Agriculture and Livestock Practices and Their Impact on the Planet

Agriculture and livestock practices essentially affect the planet, both positively and negatively. In addition to being essential for feeding the entire world's population, they also play a role in climate change, deforestation, soil erosion, the loss of biodiversity, and water pollution.

Deforestation for land transformation is perhaps the main way that agribusiness influences the planet. The Food and Agriculture Organization (FAO) states that agriculture accounts for approximately 80% of global deforestation (FAO, 2021). Not only does deforestation decrease the number of trees that take in CO2 from the atmosphere, but it also causes soil erosion, pollution of the water supply, and the loss of biodiversity. The planet's capacity to support life is significantly compromised as a result of this.

Through their digestive processes, livestock, particularly cattle, and sheep, also contribute to climate change by producing large quantities of methane. Methane is a potent greenhouse gas that has a much greater potential to cause global warming than CO2. Clearing forests and other natural habitats for livestock feed frequently necessitates deforestation and the loss of biodiversity. Moreover, nitrous oxide, another potent greenhouse gas, is released into the atmosphere when synthetic fertilizers are used in agriculture.

Another way that agriculture and livestock practices influence the planet is by using water assets. According to FAO 2021, agriculture accounts for approximately 70% of global freshwater withdrawals. Although irrigation is a common practice in agriculture, it can result in soil salinization and the loss of water, both of which have a negative impact on crop yield (FAO, 2021). A significant amount of water is also required for livestock production, both for drinking and for growing feed crops.

In particular, in regions that are already experiencing water stress as a result of climate change, the overuse of water resources in agriculture and livestock production can result in water scarcity (IPCC, 2018). To ensure the long-term use of water resources, it is essential to promote water-efficient farming methods like drip irrigation and rainwater harvesting (FAO, 2021).

The degradation of soil is another significant global effect of agricultural and livestock practices. Soil erosion, loss of soil fertility, and degradation of soil structure can result from intensive agricultural practices like excessive tillage, monoculture, and the use of synthetic pesticides and fertilizers (FAO, 2021). Not only does soil degradation have a negative impact on crop productivity but also on water quality and biodiversity.

The production of beef and dairy products makes up the majority of livestock production's contribution to approximately 14.5% of global greenhouse gas emissions, according to the Food and Agriculture Organization of the United Nations (FAO, 2013). Also, the utilization of engineered manures in agribusiness represents around 10% of worldwide ozone-harming substance emanations (EPA, 2021).

To address soil debasement, reasonable cultivating practices, for example, agroforestry, cover trimming, and edit pivot can be executed. Soil health is improved, soil erosion is reduced, and carbon is stored (FAO, 2021). Furthermore, decreasing the utilization of engineered composts and pesticides can likewise further develop soil wellbeing and diminish soil corruption.

The practices of livestock and agriculture have a significant impact on the environment. These impacts include deforestation, emissions of greenhouse gases, depletion of water resources, and degradation of soil. To mitigate these effects and ensure the long-term sustainability of agriculture and food production, it is essential to promote sustainable farming practices. We can still feed the world's population while simultaneously reducing our impact on the environment and adopting sustainable practices like regenerative agriculture.

However, there are a number of ways to lessen the environmental impact of livestock and agricultural practices. Promoting sustainable agriculture, which includes utilizing crop rotation and cover crops to improve soil health, reducing the use of synthetic pesticides and fertilizers, and implementing agroforestry practices to increase biodiversity and sequester carbon, is one strategy (FAO, 2021). Reduced meat consumption and a shift toward plant-based diets can also significantly reduce demand for livestock production, which in turn reduces greenhouse gas emissions (Ranganathan et al., 2016).

We owe it to ourselves and to society as a whole to reduce the negative effects that farming and raising livestock have on the environment. Supporting sustainable agriculture and making dietary choices that reduce meat consumption are examples of this. We can help preserve the planet for future generations by doing so.

The Role of Industrial Processes in Climate Change

One of the most significant global challenges we face right now is the acceleration of climate change, which is exacerbated by industrial processes. An industrial process is any human activity that involves the production, transportation, or consumption of goods and services. These processes heavily rely on fossil fuels, which when burned release greenhouse gases (GHGs) into the atmosphere.

According to the Intergovernmental Panel on Climate Change (IPCC) (IPCC, 2014), energy-related activities like the production of electricity and heat accounted for the majority of industrial processes' greenhouse gas (GHG) emissions in 2010. When raw materials are extracted, processed, and transported, as well as when products are produced and disposed of, GHG emissions are also produced.

One of the most significant industrial processes that contribute to climate change is the production of cement. According to the International Energy Agency (IEA), cement production results in approximately 7% of all global greenhouse gas (GHG) emissions due to the chemical reaction and high energy consumption required for the process. Other industrial processes that are significant contributors to greenhouse gas (GHG) emissions include the production of chemicals, plastics, iron, and steel.

However, industrial processes can be reduced in some ways to lessen their impact on climate change. One system is to grow the use of harmless to the ecosystem power sources, for instance, sun arranged, wind, and hydropower in the creation and transportation of work and items. According to IPCC (2014), this would assist in reducing emissions of greenhouse gases and reduce dependence on petroleum derivatives.

Another strategy is to improve the energy efficiency of industrial processes. This can be accomplished by utilizing energy management systems (EMS) in conjunction with more energy-efficient processes and equipment (IEA, 2020). In addition, the application of principles of a circular economy, in which resources are utilized for as long as possible and waste is minimized, has the potential to cut down on the quantity of raw materials required for production, thereby lowering emissions of greenhouse gases (Ellen, 2021).

Industrial processes clearly play a significant role in climate change, but there are ways to lessen their impact. By using more renewable energy, increasing energy efficiency, and adhering to the principles of the circular economy, we can work toward a more sustainable future and reduce the amount of greenhouse gas (GHG) emissions produced by industrial processes.

Urbanization and Population Growth are the Factors Contributing to Global Warming

Urbanization and population growth are two major factors that contribute to global warming. As more people move into urban areas, energy consumption, the need for transportation, and the production of waste all contribute to an increase in greenhouse gas (GHG) emissions.

As urbanization has accelerated, demand for housing, infrastructure, and commercial buildings has grown. According to IPCC (2014), this has led to an increase in development activities that make extensive use of resources and energy. Heating, cooling, and lighting account for 39% of all energy used in buildings worldwide, according to UNEP 2021. As the number of people living in cities continues to rise, eco-friendly infrastructure and buildings that use less energy will become even more important to reduce emissions of greenhouse gases.

Another significant factor in global warming is transportation. The IPCC states that as urban populations rise, so does the demand for transportation. As a result, private automobiles and public transportation are used by a greater number of people, both of which contribute to the emission of CO2 and other pollutants. According to UNEP 2021/2, the transportation industry accounts for approximately 23% of global GHG emissions. Ozone depleting substance outflows from the transportation area can be fundamentally decreased by empowering the utilization of public transportation, electric vehicles, and dynamic methods of transportation like trekking and strolling (IEA, 2021).

Waste production has also increased as a result of population growth and urbanization. Methane is one of the greenhouse gases produced when waste breaks down.

According to the Environmental Protection Agency (EPA), landfills are responsible for 18% of the global emissions of methane. Composting, using landfill gas as an energy source, and waste reduction and recycling programs all have the potential to significantly reduce greenhouse gas (GHG) emissions from waste management (EPA, 2022).

In expansion to expanding vitality proficiency, another procedure to moderate the effect of urbanization and populace development on climate alteration is to energize feasible urban advancement. This incorporates planning cities to be more walkable and bikeable, advancing open transportation, and making green spaces. Urban green spaces, such as parks and green rooftops, can offer assistance assimilate carbon dioxide and give a cooling impact, diminishing the urban warm island impact (IPCC, 2018).

Besides, advancing feasible transportation alternatives can essentially decrease nursery gas outflows. This will be accomplished through the selection of electric vehicles, the extension of open transportation frameworks, and the advancement of biking and strolling. For illustration, cities like Amsterdam and Copenhagen have effectively actualized bike-friendly foundations and arrangements, coming about in tall rates of cycling and moo rates of car utilization (Transport & Environment, 2021).

Chapter 4

Impacts of Global Warming

Human activities have instigated a phenomenon known as global warming, which is a critical environmental problem that demands urgent attention. The passage implies that there has been a gradual rise in the average temperature of the Earth's atmosphere and oceans, primarily due to the release of greenhouse gases, including carbon dioxide, methane, and nitrous oxide, from human activities such as the burning of fossil fuels, industrial processes, and deforestation. The increase of greenhouse gas levels holds heat inside the atmosphere, leading to a surge in global temperatures.

The consequences of the phenomenon of global warming have a wide-ranging effect on various aspects of both the living world and the natural surroundings. They include a rise in sea levels, melting of polar ice caps and glaciers, increased frequency and severity of extreme weather conditions, alterations in precipitation patterns, and modifications in environmental factors.

This chapter provides a comprehensive examination of how global warming is affecting the environment, economy, and human well-being. We will be investigating the present situation and potential future outlook of global warming while exploring possible solutions to lessen its effects and cope with its consequences.

The Impact of Global Warming on Ecosystems

Global warming contains a critical effect on environments around the world. Ecosystems are complex systems of living and non-living components that are interdependent and depend on a fragile adjustment to operate legitimately (Millennium Ecosystem Assessment, 2005). Changes in temperature, precipitation designs, and climate occasions can modify the adjustment of these ecosystems, leading to a wide run of negative results (IPCC, 2014). The impacts of global warming on ecosystems change from nation to nation, and these impacts can be noteworthy (Rosenzweig et al., 2008). In this segment, we'll talk about the effect of global warming on ecosystems, with a center on particular illustrations from diverse nations.

One of the foremost noteworthy impacts of global warming on ecosystems is the loss of biodiversity. As temperatures rise, many species are struggling to adjust, driving to decay in their populations (Sala et al., 2000). For illustration, within the Amazon rainforest, one of the foremost biodiverse environments in the world, rising temperatures and changes in precipitation designs are causing a decrease in plant and creature species. This, in turn, can influence the food chain, driving lopsided characteristics that can have long-term results (Parmesan, 2006).

Essentially, in Australia, global warming is causing extreme harm to the Great Barrier Reef, one of the world's most noteworthy coral reef ecosystems. Rising ocean temperatures are causing coral dying, which can eventually lead to the passing of coral colonies. This, in turn, can influence the numerous angle and other species that depend on the reef for their survival (IPCC, 2014).

In North America, global warming is causing changes within the timing of regular occasions, such as the sprouting of plants and the movement of fowl. These changes can have noteworthy impacts on ecosystems, as the timing of occasions is pivotal for keeping up the adjustment of the ecosystem (Rosenzweig et al., 2008). For illustration, within the Rocky Mountains, warmer temperatures are causing flowers to sprout prior to spring. This will influence the timing of fertilization, which can have critical impacts on the survival of pollinator species like bees and butterflies (IPCC, 2014).

In Europe, global warming is causing a decrease in Alpine ecosystems, which are domestic to numerous interesting and uncommon species. Rising temperatures are causing icy masses to liquefy, driving changes in water accessibility and soil dampness levels. This, in turn, can influence the plants and creatures that depend on these environments, eventually driving to the decay of biodiversity (Sala et al., Global biodiversity scenarios for the year 2100, 2000).

In Africa, global warming is causing changes in precipitation designs, which can influence the survival of numerous species. For case, within the Sahel locale of Africa, rising temperatures are causing droughts, which can lead to a decrease in vegetation and natural life. This, in turn, can influence the vocations of neighborhood communities that depend on these ecosystems for their survival (Le et al., 2020).

In general, the effect of global warming on ecosystems is noteworthy and shifted. It influences each portion of the world in an unexpected way, and the results can be serious. In any case, there are arrangements that can offer assistance to moderate the effect of global warming on ecosystems. These incorporate diminishing greenhouse gas emissions, securing natural habitats, and developing more feasible arrive utilize hones.

The Effects of Climate Change on Agriculture and Food Security

Climate change postures critical challenges to agriculture, food security, and provincial employments in numerous nations. Concurring to the Intergovernmental Panel on Climate Change (IPCC), the impacts of climate change on agriculture and food security incorporate changes in crop yields, crop quality, and food costs, as well as changes in bugs and infections. These impacts are especially serious in nations where agriculture is the most source of income and where the agricultural division is profoundly subordinate to precipitation.

Africa is one of the regions most powerless to the impacts of climate change on agriculture and food security. For illustration, in West Africa, climate change is causing changes in precipitation designs, which are influencing crop yields and food security. Dione et al. (2020) note that farmers in this locale are battling to adjust to changing rainfall patterns which are often affecting their vocations. In expansion, the IPCC (2014) notes that climate alteration is causing an increment in bothers and maladies in some African nations, which is influencing crop yields.

In Asia, climate change is additionally having a noteworthy affect on agriculture and food security. For case, in India, climate change is causing changes in monsoon precipitation designs, which are affecting crop yields and food security. According to the Food and Agriculture Organization (FAO), climate change is additionally causing an increment in extraordinary climate occasions, such as dry spells and surges, which are influencing agriculture and food security in many Asian nations.

Latin America is another region where the impacts of climate change on agriculture and food security are getting to be progressively apparent. According to (Le et al., 2020), climate change is causing changes in rainfall designs in numerous Latin American countries, which are influencing crop yields and food security. In addition, the IPCC (2014) notes that climate change is causing an increment in bugs and infections in a few Latin American nations, which is influencing crop yields.

The impacts of climate change on agriculture and food security are not restricted to developing nations. In developed countries, such as the United States and Australia, climate change is additionally having an impact on agriculture and food security. For example, within the United States, climate change is causing an increment in extraordinary climate occasions, such as dry spells and surges, which are influencing crop yields and food costs (Rosenzweig et al., 2008). In addition, climate change is causing changes in precipitation designs in a few ranges, which are influencing crop yields and food security.

In order to adjust to the impacts of climate change on agriculture and food security, numerous nations are actualizing methodologies to make strides in their flexibility. These methodologies incorporate the development of drought-resistant crop assortments, the execution of water system frameworks, and the advancement of early caution frameworks for bugs and infections. Be that as it may, these techniques are not continuously viable, and there's a requirement for advanced research and improvement in this zone.

Climate change is having a significant affect on agriculture and food security in numerous nations around the world. The impacts are especially serious in developing nations where agriculture is the most source of income and where the agricultural segment is profoundly dependent on rainfall. To address these impacts, there's a requirement for the expanded venture in inquiry about and advancement, as well as the execution of methodologies to move forward the flexibility of rural frameworks.

The Impact of Sea Level Rise and Coastal Flooding on Cities and Communities

Ocean levels are rising essentially as a result of the softening of ice sheets and icy masses caused by rising global temperatures (Church & White, 2011). Ocean-level rise and coastal flooding will have an obliterating impact on our towns and cities (IPCC, 2019). Concurring to (Nelson et al., 2020). The combination of rising ocean levels and storm surges can result in coastal flooding that causes harm to frameworks, homes, and businesses. Ocean level rise features a more noteworthy potential to have an affect on coastal cities and communities, and low-lying island countries are especially at hazard (IPCC, 2019).

Agreeing to IPCC (2019), the annihilating impacts of rising ocean levels on our cities and communities are getting to be progressively clear. Coastal flooding can result in infrastructure harm, such as streets, buildings, and bridges, as ocean levels proceed to rise (Nelson et al., 2020). In expansion, saltwater interruption into coastal groundwater can hurt horticulture, sully drinking water sources, and affect our way of life (IPCC, 2019). Angling individuals bunch can moreover be truly affected by the impact of the sea level climb (UNDP, 2020). For occasion, saltwater interruption has polluted freshwater sources in Bangladesh, rendering them unpalatable for drinking and water system, coming about in noteworthy edit misfortunes and nourishment deficiencies (Ali, 2021).

Also, businesses and economies can be altogether affected by coastal flooding, influencing not as it were our implies of subsistence but to the GDP of our countries (IPCC, 2019). Ocean-side locales within the US, for illustration, make up more than 45% of the nation's GDP (Net household item), with ranges, for case, the travel industry and angling contributing in a general sense (NOAA, 2020). Businesses may be constrained to near or migrate as a result of flooding and foundation harm as a result of ocean level rise's affect on coastal communities (IPCC, 2019).

Sea level rise encompasses an especially negative affect on low-lying island countries (IPCC, 2019). Ocean level rise is as of now having an impact on Pacific Sea countries like Kiribati and Tuvalu, causing saltwater intrusion, coastal disintegration, and flooding (UNDP, 2020). Rising ocean levels seem to result in the misfortune of all of these nations' landmasses, uprooting their whole population (IPCC, 2019).

Luckily, cities all over the world are taking steps to decrease the impacts of coastal flooding and rising ocean levels. For occasion, Miami-Dade District (Miami-Dade District, 2020) reports that the city of Miami, Florida, has actualized a number of measures to watch against coastal flooding. These incorporate raising streets and buildings, developing seawalls, and extending green spaces that can assimilate stormwater. Based on its long history of managing flooding, the Netherlands has developed advanced water administration frameworks like dams and embankments as well as the creation of unused arrive through arrival recovery (Netherlands Undertaking Organization, 2020).

The impacts of coastal flooding and rising ocean levels on our cities and communities cannot be disregarded (IPCC, 2019). Cities around the world are too at the chance, but low-lying island countries are especially defenseless (UNDP, 2020). Concurring to IPCC (2019), the harm to economies, homes, businesses, and the framework can be noteworthy. In any case, we are ready to moderate the impacts of rising ocean levels by developing seawalls, hoisting frameworks, and constructing sophisticated water administration frameworks. We must take prompt action to moderate the impacts of coastal flooding and rising ocean levels on our economies and communities.

The Human Health Effects of Climate Change

Climate change includes a critical affect on human health, with rising global temperatures influencing helpless populations around the world. Presentation to extraordinary warm, discuss contamination, and extraordinary climate occasions can lead to a extend of health issues, counting respiratory ailments, cardiovascular infections, and warm stroke. In expansion, changes in temperature and precipitation designs can lead to the spread of infectious diseases and vector-borne sicknesses, such as malaria, dengue fever, and Zika infection.

Studies have appeared that discuss contamination caused by burning fossil fills contributes to over 3 million untimely passings universally each year (World Health Organization, 2018). In cities like Delhi, India, where discuss contamination levels are reliably tall, the rate of respiratory ailments and cardiovascular illnesses is tall. Moreover, global warming has expanded the recurrence and seriousness of heat waves, which can cause warm fatigue, heatstroke, and indeed passing, especially among defenseless populations.

The impacts of climate change on human health can be seen in numerous nations around the world. In India, extraordinary heat waves have driven an increment in heat-related ailments and passings, especially among vulnerable populations such as the elderly and those living in destitution. In expansion, discuss contamination, exacerbated by the utilization of fossil powers and transportation outflows, has driven an increment in respiratory sicknesses and cardiovascular infections.

In Africa, changes in temperature and precipitation designs have driven to the spread of irresistible maladies and vector-borne ailments, such as malaria and dengue fever. The World Health Organization (2018) estimates that over 200 million individuals in Africa are at hazard of malaria, which is transmitted by mosquitoes and is delicate to climatic changes such as temperature and precipitation. Additionally, extraordinary climate occasions, such as surges and dry spells, can lead to a lack of healthy sustenance and nourishment uncertainty, which can have long-term impacts on health (IPCC, 2014).

In the United States, extraordinary heatwaves have too driven to an increment in heat-related ailments and passings, especially in urban zones where the urban warm island impact is more conspicuous. Concurring to the Centers for Disease Control and Prevention (CDC, 2018), heatwaves caused over 7,200 passings in the US between 1999 and 2010. In expansion, changes in temperature and precipitation designs have driven an increment within the predominance of Lyme infection and other vector-borne ailments within the Northeastern United States.

Children, the elderly, and those with pre-existing health conditions are especially helpless to the impacts of climate change. In expansion, marginalized communities, such as low-income populations and indigenous communities, are regularly excessively influenced by the health impacts of climate change due to variables such as the need to get to healthcare and the presentation of natural risks (IPCC, 2014).

In reaction to this issue, nations and communities must take action to decrease greenhouse gas outflows and advance public health to relieve the affect of climate change on human health.

One solution to address the health impacts of climate change is to extend venture in healthcare frameworks and move forward get to healthcare for helpless populations. This will incorporate giving healthcare administrations in inaccessible and marginalized zones, as well as contributing in preventative measures such as immunizations and malady observation programs (World Health Organization, 2021). By doing so, communities can diminish the frequency of climate-related ailments and guarantee that everybody has get to the care they require.

Another solution is to advance sustainable transportation and vitality proficiency. The European Union has set targets to diminish greenhouse gas outflows by at slightest 40% by 2030, and has executed approaches to advance sustainable transportation and vitality proficiency (European Commission, 2021). This incorporates contributing to renewable vitality sources and advancing the utilization of open transportation and cycling. By doing so, nations can decrease their carbon footprint and promote public health by decreasing discuss contamination.

Cities can also actualize measures to diminish the urban warm island impact, such as planting trees and making green spaces (UN-Habitat, 2021). These measures can offer assistance to diminish the affect of extraordinarily warm occasions on vulnerable populations, especially in urban ranges. By making more green spaces, cities can also make strides to discuss quality and advance physical activity, which can have positive impacts on public health.

Further to these measures, it is critical for nations and communities to work together to address the root causes of climate change. By diminishing greenhouse gas emissions and advancing feasible improvements, we are able to mitigate the affect of climate alter on human health. This could incorporate advancing the utilization of renewable vitality sources, diminishing squandering and advancing reusing, and contributing to green innovations (United Nations, 2021).

The Economic Impacts of Global Warming

Climate change is one of the foremost squeezing issues of our time, with critical and far-reaching financial impacts that influence businesses, governments, and people around the world. Global warming, the most driver of climate change, is causing rising temperatures, sea-level rise, and changes in precipitation designs, among other impacts. These changes are as of now having major economic impacts, such as expanded costs for infrastructure support and repairs, decreased agricultural efficiency, and expanded recurrence and seriousness of common catastrophes. In this setting, it's vital to get it the economic impacts of global warming and to distinguish potential solutions to mitigate these impacts.

One of the foremost significant economic impacts of global warming is its impact on horticulture. Rising temperatures and changes in precipitation designs can lead to decreased crop yields, which in turn can lead to higher food costs and expanded food frailty. extraordinary climate occasions such as surges, dry seasons, and heatwaves can also harm crops and infrastructure, driving to noteworthy economic misfortunes for agriculturists and other stakeholders within the agricultural division (IPCC, 2018).

Another major economic affect of climate change is its impact on the energy division. As temperatures rise, request for cooling increments, which can lead to higher energy consumption and expanded strain on energy foundation. extreme climate occasions such as typhoons, storms, and wildfires can harm energy foundation, driving to power blackouts and supply disturbances. This, in turn, can lead to higher vitality costs and decreased financial efficiency (USGCRP, 2018).

The impacts of climate change are also likely to be felt within the tourism industry, which is especially defenseless to changes in climate designs and ocean levels. Rising temperatures can lead to a decay in snow-based tourism, whereas sea-level rise can lead to the disintegration of shorelines and coastal framework, decreasing the engaging quality of tourist goals. In expansion, extreme climate occasions such as tropical storms and surges can disturb travel and cause noteworthy economic misfortunes for businesses that depend on tourism (UNEP, 2017).

The transportation sector is another area of the economy that's likely to be influenced by climate change. Higher temperatures can lead to an increment in air pollution, which can have negative health impacts and lead to expanded healthcare costs. moreover, extreme climate occasions such as surges and storms can damage transportation foundation, driving to disturbances within the supply chain and higher transportation costs (UNFCCC, 2019).

The monetary division is additionally helpless to the impacts of climate alter. As the dangers related with climate change become more clear, financial specialists are likely to become more cautious approximately contributing in companies and industries that are exceedingly uncovered to climate-related dangers. Further, protections companies may confront higher costs as a result of expanded claims related to climate-related occasions such as surges and rapidly spreading fires (G20, 2021).

In addition to the economic impacts of global warming that we examined prior, it's critical to note that there are also potential solutions that can offer assistance moderate the negative impacts of climate change on the economy. These solutions incorporate both relief measures, which point to decrease greenhouse gas outflows, and adaptation measures, which point to assist communities and businesses adjust to the impacts of climate change.

One key solution to moderating the financial impacts of climate change is to move to a low-carbon economy. This would include lessening greenhouse gas emissions by contributing in renewable energy sources such as sun powered, wind, and geothermal control, as well as increasing energy productivity in buildings and transportation. Transitioning to a low-carbon economy seem make modern economic opportunities, such as occupations in the renewable energy division and expanded development in clean vitality innovations (IPCC, 2018).

Another solution to mitigating the economic impacts of climate change is to contribute in adaptation measures. These measures might incorporate foundation changes such as ocean dividers and surge boundaries to ensure against sea-level rise and flooding, as well as advancements to transportation systems to decrease the impacts of extreme climate occasions. Contributing in investigate and improvement of climate-resilient crops may offer assistance agriculturists adapt to changing climate patterns and ensure against crop disappointments (USGCRP, 2018).

Another imperative solution to relieving the economic impacts of climate change is to advance maintainable arrive utilize hones. This might include diminishing deforestation and advancing reforestation, as well as advancing economical agricultural practices such as no-till cultivating and agroforestry. These hones can help sequester carbon in soils and vegetation, diminishing greenhouse gas emissions and advancing soil wellbeing (UNEP, 2017).

At last, it's critical to note that addressing the economic impacts of global warming will require a facilitated exertion from governments, businesses, and individuals. Governments can play a key role in setting policies and directions that incentivize the transition to a low-carbon economy and promote adjustment measures. Businesses can also play a key part in diminishing greenhouse gas emanations and contributing in clean energy advances. People can moreover take action to decrease their possess carbon impression by making changes to their lifestyle, such as decreasing energy utilization, utilizing public transportation, and lessening meat utilization (UNFCCC, 2019).

Whereas the economic impacts of global warming are noteworthy and wide-ranging, there are moreover potential solutions that can offer assistance mitigate these impacts. These arrangements incorporate transitioning to a low-carbon economy, contributing in adjustment measures, advancing feasible land use hones, and taking action at the person level. By working together to address the financial impacts of climate change, able to offer assistance to guarantee a more maintainable and prosperous future for all.

Countries Around the World Affected by Climate Impacts

Every country on the planet is affected by climate change, which is a global problem. No country is immune to the effects of rising temperatures, sea level rise and changing weather patterns, despite the fact that some regions are more vulnerable to climate change than others. We will explore the ways in which different countries around the world are responding to the effects of climate change.

The economy and natural environment in the United States have been severely affected by climate change. With more than 5 million people living within 4 feet of sea level rise, coastal areas are particularly vulnerable to sea level rise. Agriculture, energy production, and public health are also affected by more intense and frequent heat waves and wildfires (USGCRP, 2018). The U.S. government has taken a number of actions to address these impacts, including setting emissions reduction targets and investing in renewable energy technologies (EPA, 2021).

Climate change is also having a significant impact in Europe, particularly in the Mediterranean. The region experiences harsher and more frequent dry seasons, affecting agricultural and water assets. Wildfires and landslides are also more likely as heat waves and floods become more frequent. The European Union is investing in renewable energy and energy efficiency to address these impacts (EEA, 2020) and setting ambitious emission reduction targets.

Agriculture and water resources in South Asia are being strongly impacted by climate change. Changing weather conditions lead to more frequent and severe floods and dry seasons, affecting food and occupational security. Low-lying countries such as Bangladesh and the Maldives are particularly concerned about rising sea levels. Governments in the region are investing in climate-resilient infrastructure and promoting methods. eco-friendly farming to minimize these impacts (ADB, 2019).

Water resources and food security are being strongly impacted in Africa by climate change. In many parts of the continent, droughts are getting worse and more frequent, leading to crop failure and increasing the risk of famine. The risk of heat and disease increases affecting public health. African governments are investing in climate-resilient infrastructure, renewable energy and sustainable land-use practices to address these impacts (AfDB, 2020).

In the Pacific Islands, environmental change is a significant danger to regular staff and people. Sea level rise alters freshwater availability, erodes coastlines and increases the likelihood of flooding. More intense and persistent storms are damaging foundations and affecting livelihoods. Governments in the region are working to reduce greenhouse gas emissions, promote sustainable fisheries, and invest in climate-resilient infrastructure to cope with these impacts (SPREP, 2021).

Australia is one of the countries most at risk from the effects of climate change. Rising temperatures, more frequent and severe droughts will increase the likelihood of wildfires and crop failures. Additionally, coastal communities, especially those in the northern regions of the country, are particularly concerned about rising sea levels. The Australian government is investing in renewable energy technologies such as wind and solar energy to mitigate these impacts (Ministry of Environment and Energy, 2021).

India is another country that is severely affected by climate change, especially in terms of weather changes and extreme weather events such as floods and droughts. The risk of waterborne diseases and heat stress increases as a result of these impacts, while also affecting agriculture, water resources and public health. The Government of India is working to reduce emissions, invest in renewable energy and use energy efficiently, and promote environmentally friendly agricultural practices to mitigate these impacts (Government of India, 2021).

Climate change is also having an impact on Pakistan, including more severe and frequent droughts and floods. The risk of food insecurity and displacement increases as a result of these impacts, affecting agriculture and water resources. The Government of Pakistan is working to reduce greenhouse gas emissions and is investing in climate change adaptation infrastructure to deal with these impacts (Government of Pakistan, 2020).

Another country that is particularly vulnerable to the effects of climate change is Bangladesh, where rising sea levels and more severe and frequent storms affecting coastal communities make this country special. vulnerable. Agriculture and water resources are also being adversely affected by changing weather conditions, leading to more severe and frequent floods and droughts. In response to these impacts, the government of Bangladesh is investing resources in environmentally sound facilities and promoting economic repetition of land use, while trying to reduce emissions of hazardous substances. ozone layer depletion (Legislature of Bangladesh, 2021).

The countries of the Middle East, especially those in the Gulf, are also being affected by environmental changes, with rising temperatures and changing atmospheric conditions posing the risk of severe stress. and increasing water scarcity. Coastal communities are affected by sea level rise, especially in low-lying countries such as Bahrain and the United Arab Emirates. To address these impacts, local legislatures are investing resources in environmentally responsible energy and electricity productivity, as well as promoting measures to protect water resources and conserve land. savings (GCC, 2018).

In the face of unnatural climate change, countries around the world are making various efforts to reduce the release of ozone-depleting substances and promote maneuvers. economic improvement.

The Australian government has developed a climate solution package that includes investments in renewable energy and technology save energy, as well as encourage farmers to adopt sustainable land use practices (Australian Department of

Environment and Energy, 2021). The goal is to reduce emissions to 26-28% below 2005 levels by 2030.

The Government of India has developed a National Action Plan on Climate Change, which includes investing in renewable energy and energy efficiency, and promoting sustainable agricultural practices (Government of India). Government of India, 2021). In addition, the government has set a target to reduce the emission intensity of GDP from he 2005 level of 33 to 35 levels by 2030.

The Government of Pakistan has developed a National Climate Change Policy that includes investing in climate-resilient infrastructure and promoting sustainable land use practices (Pakistan Government, 2020). Additionally, the government has set a target to reduce emissions to 20 normal levels by 2030. Bangladesh:

The Government of Bangladesh has developed a Climate Change Strategy and Action Plan which includes investing in climate resilient infrastructure and promoting sustainable land use practices. In addition, the government has set a target of reducing he five emissions to normal levels by 2030 (Bangladesh Government, 2021).

Middle Eastern Countries: Governments in the Middle East have set various targets to reduce outflows and promote environmentally friendly energy, for example, Saudi Arabia's target The youngest is to produce half of its electricity from renewables by 2030 and the United Arab Emirates in the Middle East. target to generate half of electricity from clean energy sources by 2050 (GCC, 2018). To address the effects of water scarcity, regional governments are also investing in water conservation technologies and promoting sustainable land use practices.

The impacts of climate change are clearly worldwide and all nations must act to combat them. A climate adjustment system has been actualized and renewable vitality innovation ventures have been propelled by governments around the world to relieve the impacts of climate change. In any case, extra endeavors are required and everybody can contribute to tackling this crisis.

Chapter 5

Mitigating Climate Change

The Role of Renewable Energy in Decrement Greenhouse Gas Emissions

As we proceed to grapple with the approaching danger of climate change, the need for elective, feasible energy sources has become progressively clear. Renewable energy, such as sun-powered, wind, and hydropower, has been touted as a promising solution for mitigating greenhouse gas emanations and lessening our dependence on fossil fuels. In this segment, we'll investigate the part of renewable energy in mitigating climate change and diminishing greenhouse gas emissions.

Renewable energy sources, such as solar and wind control, have picked up significant footing in recent years as practical alternatives to conventional fossil fuels. The International Energy Agency reports that renewable energy accounted for 72% of global control extension in 2019 (International Energy Agency, 2020). One of the primary preferences of renewable energy is that it produces small to no greenhouse gas outflows, subsequently moderating the antagonistic impacts of climate change. In truth, a study conducted by the National Renewable Energy Laboratory found that the widespread selection of renewable energy sources might possibly diminish greenhouse gas emanations by up to 80% by 2050.

Besides, renewable energy sources are getting to be progressively cost-competitive with conventional fossil fuels. A report by the International Renewable Energy Agency (IRENA) found that the cost of renewable energy has declined by 80% over the past decade (IRENA, 2019). This fetched decrease has made renewable energy more accessible and financially attainable for both created and developing nations.

In spite of these preferences, there are still challenges that must be addressed to completely realize the potential of renewable energy in moderating climate alter. One of the essential challenges is the irregular nature of a few renewable energy sources, such as wind and solar control. These sources are dependent on outside components, such as climate conditions, and may not deliver energy reliably. In any case, advancements in energy storage advances and network integration are making a difference to address these challenges.

Another challenge is the require for significant infrastructure speculation to back the widespread adoption of renewable energy. This incorporates creating modern transmission lines, storage facilities, and other vital framework to back the integration of renewable energy into existing control frameworks (IRENA, 2019). However, with the proceeded decay in renewable energy costs and the expanding urgency of the climate emergency, numerous nations are contributing intensely in renewable energy framework.

Renewable energy has become an progressively critical component of global endeavors to moderate climate change. In addition to the natural benefits, renewable energy has the potential to stimulate economic development and make modern job opportunities. According to a report by the International Renewable Energy Agency (IRENA), the renewable energy division utilized 11.5 million individuals globally in 2019, representing a 6% increment from the past year (IRENA, 2020). The report also ventures that the renewable energy sector might utilize up to 42 million people by 2050.

Moreover, renewable energy can advance energy security and autonomy by diminishing dependence on remote energy sources. In numerous nations, fossil fuel imports are a noteworthy deplete on national budgets, and renewable energy can offer assistance to decrease these costs (IRENA, 2019). Moreover, renewable energy sources are regularly more versatile to disturbances, such as natural catastrophes or geopolitical conflicts, than conventional fossil fuels.

One of the foremost promising renewable energy sources is solar power. Solar energy is abundant and broadly distributed, with the potential to supply energy to even the most remote regions of the world. According to the International Energy Agency, solar power is the cheapest source of power in history in some regions (International Energy Agency, 2020). Advances in solar panel innovation and manufacturing have led to significant cost decreases in recent years, making solar energy more accessible and cost-effective than ever before.

Wind power is another important renewable energy source. Wind turbines can be conveyed on arrive or at ocean and are able of producing expansive sums of power. According to the Global Wind Energy Council, the worldwide wind power capacity reached 743 GW in 2020, a 53 GW increment from the past year (Global Wind Energy Council, 2021). Wind power has the potential to play a significant part in decreasing greenhouse gas emanations and advancing a sustainable energy future.
Different countries have implemented different arrangements and initiatives to advance the utilization of renewable energy sources and diminish greenhouse gas emanations.

For example, China has ended up a global pioneer in renewable energy, contributing intensely to wind and solar power. In 2020, China added 72 GW of new solar power capacity, accounting for nearly half of the world's modern solar establishments (International Energy Agency, 2021). The Chinese government has moreover set yearning targets for the advancement of renewable energy, pointing to reaching 1,200 GW of introduced capacity by 2030 (National Energy Administration, 2021).

Essentially, India has made critical strides in advancing renewable energy, especially in the shape of solar power. In 2020, India was the third-largest solar market in the world, including 4.1 GW of modern solar capacity (International Energy Agency, 2021). The Indian government has moreover set a target of accomplishing 450 GW of renewable energy capacity by 2030, with solar control accounting for a noteworthy parcel of this objective (Ministry of New and Renewable Energy, 2021).

In Europe, a few nations have set driven targets for renewable energy appropriation. For example, Sweden points to become carbon impartial by 2045 and has already accomplished critical advance in decreasing greenhouse gas emanations through the utilize of renewable energy sources (Swedish Energy Agency, 2021). Germany has also made noteworthy ventures in renewable energy, especially in wind power, and points to have a 65% share of renewable energy in power utilization by 2030 (Federal Ministry for Economic Affairs and Energy, 2021).

Within the United States, several states have executed renewable portfolio benchmarks, which require a certain rate of power to be created from renewable sources. California, for illustration, has set a target of creating 100% of its power from renewable sources by 2045 (California Energy Commission, 2021). The federal government has also reported plans to contribute intensely in renewable energy, with a objective of accomplishing a carbon-free power segment by 2035 (The White House, 2021).

Generally, diverse nations have executed different arrangements and activities to advance the adoption of renewable energy sources and diminish greenhouse gas outflows. Whereas there's still much work to be done, these endeavors represent a critical step towards a more sustainable and climate-friendly energy future.

The Importance of Energy Efficiency and Conservation

Climate change is a complex issue that requires a multifaceted approach to mitigate its impacts. The utilization of renewable energy sources, energy effectiveness and conservation can play a critical role in decreasing greenhouse gas emanations. The International Energy Agency (IEA) estimates that energy productivity measures may diminish global greenhouse gas emissions by up to 12.7 gigatons of CO_2 by 2050, which is proportionate to the current yearly emanations of the European Union and the United States combined (IEA, 2019).

The execution of energy effectiveness and conservation measures can be seen over the globe. For instance, the European Union has built up driven targets to decrease energy consumption and increment energy efficiency. In 2018, the EU embraced the Clean Energy for All Europeans bundle, which sets authoritative targets for energy productivity, renewable energy, and greenhouse gas decreases. The bundle incorporates measures such as energy labeling, eco-design, and energy execution guidelines for buildings, machines, and vehicles (European Commission, 2019).

Japan has executed a range of energy efficiency measures, including the Best Runner Program, which sets energy efficiency standards for a wide extend of items and gear. The program has been effective in advancing the improvement and appropriation of energy-efficient innovations, and it is evaluated to have decreased Japan's CO_2 emanations by around 13 million tons in 2018 (Ministry of Economy, Trade and Industry, 2019).

In the United States, energy efficiency measures have been implemented at both the government and state levels. The Energy Policy Act of 2005, for example, built up energy efficiency guidelines for a assortment of items, counting apparatuses and lighting. Moreover, numerous states have actualized their claim energy efficiency programs and approaches, including building codes, utility energy effectiveness programs, and assess motivating forces (U.S. Department of Energy, 2020).

In spite of the advance made in executing energy effectiveness and preservation measures, there are still significant opportunities for advancement. The IEA estimates that the global potential for energy efficiency advancements is proportionate to approximately 40% of current global energy requests (IEA, 2019).

Energy effectiveness and preservation measures are not only critical for diminishing greenhouse gas emissions, but they can moreover bring various benefits to society and the economy. For instance, progressing the energy effectiveness of buildings can lead to lower energy bills for homeowners and businesses, while also making occupations within the development and energy sectors. In reality, the IEA estimates that energy effectiveness enhancements might make up to 9.8 million employments globally by 2050 (IEA, 2019).

Moreover, energy efficiency and preservation can also improve energy security by reducing reliance on imported fossil fuels. This will improve energy autonomy and flexibility, especially for nations that are intensely dependent on energy imports. For instance, the United States has been able to decrease its dependence on remote oil by executing energy effectiveness measures and expanding domestic production of oil and gas (U.S. Energy Information Administration, 2021).

In addition to these benefits, energy proficiency and preservation measures can also contribute to poverty reduction and social improvement. Progressed access to energy-efficient appliances and innovations can diminish energy bills for low-income families, liberating up reserves for other fundamental needs. Besides, energy effectiveness measures in buildings can progress indoor discuss quality and consolation, which can have positive impacts on public health and well-being (IEA, 2019).

In general, the significance of energy effectiveness and preservation measures in moderating climate change cannot be overstated. While progress has been made in implementing these measures over the globe, there's still significant potential for advancement. Subsequently, proceeded venture in energy efficiency and preservation measures should be a key priority for governments, businesses, and people as part of a comprehensive approach to building a maintainable and versatile future.

Methods for Reducing Emissions from Transportation and Industry

Lessening greenhouse gas outflows from the transport and industrial divisions is fundamental to relieving climate change. These divisions account for a critical share of global emanations and require a range of policies and advances to decrease them. This area audits a few methods utilized to decrease emanations from transport and industry.

One procedure for diminishing transport outflows is to switch to low-carbon fuels and vehicles. These incorporate electric vehicles, hydrogen fuel cell vehicles, and biofuels. These choices can essentially diminish emissions, particularly when fueled by renewable energy sources. However, sending low-carbon vehicles and framework requires significant venture and steady measures to overcome advertising boundaries and drive appropriation (IEA, 2021).

Another approach to diminishing transport-related emanations is mobility administration, aimed at moving forward the effectiveness of transport frameworks. These incorporate techniques such as public transport, carpooling, biking, and strolling. Empowering and encouraging the utilization of public transport and dynamic mobility can diminish the number of vehicles on the street, subsequently lessening emanations and improving discuss quality. Moreover, mobility administration can offer assistance alleviate congestion, saving commuters and businesses time and money (ITDP, 2019).

Within the industrial division, decreasing emanations requires improving energy efficiency, adopting low-carbon energy sources, and conveying carbon capture and storage (CCS) advances. Energy efficiency measures offer assistance to reduce energy utilization and costs while lessening emanations. Low-carbon energy sources such as renewables and nuclear control can give carbon-free power for industrial forms. CCS innovation, on the other hand, can capture and store carbon emanations from industrial forms and anticipate them from being discharged into the environment (IEA, 2020). Circular economy approaches help diminish outflows from the industry by advancing asset efficiency and decreasing squandering. This approach incorporates developing products and processes to minimize asset utilization, reuse materials, and products, and recycle squander. By decreasing requests for new materials and energy, the circular economy can help diminish emissions and decrease the environmental impact of mechanical exercises (Ellen MacArthur Foundation, 2021).

Concurring to the International Energy Agency (IAEA), 2020, transportation and industry account for around 28% and 21% of global outflows, respectively. Thusly, it is critical to track down effective methods to reduce outpourings from these zones.

According to (Fagnant & Kockelman, 2015), electric vehicles (EVs) transmit significantly less carbon dioxide than gasoline-powered vehicles. Moreover, the transportation industry is progressively turning to hydrogen as a fuel since it can be delivered from renewable sources and only produces water vapor when utilized as a fuel (Samsatli et al., 2018). In any case, the selection of these low-carbon fuels requires critical infrastructure and innovation ventures, which may display a challenge for a few countries and divisions.

Advancing dynamic transportation modes like cycling, strolling, and public transportation is another way to cut down on outflows from transportation. Agreeing with Kong & Cho (2019), this may lead to a diminishment in the number of single-occupancy vehicles on the road. Moreover, low-emission zones and arrangements like clog charging can energize the utilization of low-emission transportation alternatives (Litman, 2020).

Energy efficiency measures have the potential to essentially cut outflows within the industrial sector. Utilizing more energy-efficient equipment and reusing squandered waste heat, for instance, can diminish energy utilization and emanations in industrial forms (International Energy Agency, 2020). Also, the industrial sector's outflows can be diminished by utilizing renewable energy sources like solar and wind power (Nordborg & Karlsson, 2019).

Furthermore, carbon capture, utilization, and storage (CCUS) advances can potentially decrease industrial emanations (Bui et al., 2018). Carbon dioxide emanations from industrial processes are captured, put away in topographical formations, or utilized in industrial forms as a portion of CCUS. This development can altogether diminish radiations from businesses like concrete, steel, and synthetic creation.

Moderating climate change requires bringing down industry and transportation emanations. CCUS advances, energy proficiency measures, and low-carbon fuels are fair some cases of the approaches that can be taken to cut outflows in these industries. However, the adoption of these methodologies requires considerable infrastructure and innovation ventures as well as the execution of directions and policies that are steady. By collaborating as a worldwide neighborhood range, we will execute compelling procedures to moderate the impacts of natural change and ensure a reasonable future for all.

The Potential of Carbon Capture and Storage Technologies

Carbon capture and storage (CCS) innovations are rising as a significant solution to relieve greenhouse gas (GHG) emanations and combat climate change. CCS advances can capture carbon dioxide (CO2) emanations from different sources, such as power plants, industries, and even the environment, and store them permanently in topographical formations or utilize them in industrial forms. we are going to examine the potential of CCS innovations and their role in diminishing GHG emanations.

The International Energy Agency (IEA) estimates that CCS technologies can contribute to around 15% of the overall GHG outflows reductions required to achieve the Paris Agreement's objective of constraining global warming to below 2°C. CCS can also play a crucial part in accomplishing net-zero outflows by 2050. According to the IEA's Sustainable Development Scenario, CCS deployment ought to reach around 7 gigatons (Gt) of CO2 per year by 2030 and increase to 15 Gt per year by 2040 and 20 Gt per year by 2050 to attain net-zero emanations (IEA, 2020).

One of the foremost critical benefits of CCS technologies is their capacity to capture CO2 emanations from different sources, such as power plants, industrial forms, and even the environment. Captured CO2 can be transported and stored in topographical formations, such as drained oil and gas supplies or saline aquifers, where it can be securely stored for thousands of years. This process can offer assistance prevent CO2 emanations from entering the climate, subsequently lessening the concentration of GHGs within the atmosphere and mitigating climate change.

CCS innovations can moreover play a vital role in the decarbonization of industries that are troublesome to zap or move to low-carbon energy sources, such as the cement, steel, and chemical industries. These industries are dependable for a critical share of global GHG outflows and require new innovations and solutions to decrease their emanations. CCS technologies can capture CO2 emissions from industrial forms and store them permanently, diminishing their carbon footprint and contributing to the decarbonization of these industries (IEA, 2020).

Moreover, CCS technologies can empower negative outflows, which are fundamental to achieving net-zero outflows. Negative emanations allude to the evacuation of CO2 from the environment, and CCS can play a significant role in accomplishing this goal. By capturing CO2 outflows from the environment and storing them forever in geological formations, CCS technologies can evacuate CO2 from the atmosphere, making a difference to moderate climate change (IPCC, 2018).

However, CCS innovations also confront noteworthy challenges, such as tall costs, specialized achievability, and public acknowledgment. The tall costs of CCS technologies have been a significant barrier to their arrangement, as they require noteworthy ventures in infrastructure and innovation development. In any case, with expanding bolster from governments and the private division, the costs of CCS technologies are anticipated to decrease in the future (IEA, 2020).

Besides, the specialized possibility of CCS innovations has been a challenge, particularly in terms of their efficiency and versatility. However, progressing investigations and advancements are improving the execution of CCS technologies, making them more effective and adaptable. For example, analysts are investigating the utilization of novel materials, such as metal-organic systems, for CO2 capture and creating new capacity methods, such as the infusion of CO2 into basalt formations (National Renewable Energy Laboratory, 2021).

At last, public acknowledgment of CCS technologies has been a significant barrier to their deployment. Many individuals are skeptical of CCS innovations, and there are concerns about their security and potential environmental impacts. However, with effective communication and engagement with stakeholders, public acceptance of CCS technologies can be made strides. For example, involving local communities in the decision-making handle and addressing their concerns can help construct beliefs and bolster CCS ventures (International Energy Agency, 2020).

In spite of the challenges, CCS advances have picked up critical support from governments and the private sector. In recent years, numerous nations have announced plans to contribute to CCS advances as part of their climate strategies. For example, the European Union has set a target to become climate-neutral by 2050 and plans to convey at least 10 gigawatts (GW) of CCS by 2030 and 40 GW by 2050. In the United States, the Biden administration has proposed significant speculations in CCS advances as part of its arrangement to achieve net-zero outflows by 2050.

Besides, the private sector has moreover appeared to expand intrigued by CCS innovations, recognizing their potential in mitigating GHG emissions and contributing to the transition to a low-carbon economy. Many companies, especially in the energy and industrial sectors, have reported plans to contribute to CCS innovations and create new ventures. For example, in September 2020, BP announced its aspiration to become a net-zero company by 2050 and plans to contribute around $5 billion in low-carbon technologies, counting CCS.

In conclusion, CCS technologies have gigantic potential in moderating GHG outflows and combating climate change. CCS can capture CO_2 emissions from different sources and store them forever, diminishing the concentration of GHGs in the environment and empowering the decarbonization of businesses that are troublesome to energize. Moreover, CCS can empower negative emanations, contributing to the accomplishment of net-zero outflows. However, the arrangement of CCS technologies faces noteworthy challenges, such as tall costs, specialized achievability, and public acknowledgment. Addressing these challenges requires collaboration between governments, the private sector, and a respectful society, as well as successful communication and engagement with stakeholders.

The Role of Policy and International Cooperation in Mitigating Climate Change

Climate change is a global challenge that requires collective activity from governments, the private division, and individuals. Policies and international cooperation play a vital role in relieving climate change by diminishing greenhouse gas (GHG) emissions and promoting sustainable development. we will examine the role of policy and international cooperation in relieving climate change.

The Paris Agreement, adopted in 2015 by 195 nations, is a landmark international agreement aimed at constraining global warming to well below 2°C above pre-industrial levels and seeking endeavors to constrain the temperature increase to 1.5°C. The Paris Agreement recognizes the critical requirement for collective action to combat climate change and calls for nationally determined contributions (NDCs) from all nations to decrease GHG emanations. NDCs are the commitments made by nations to diminish their GHG outflows and adapt to the impacts of climate change.

Policies play a basic role in advancing the selection of low-carbon innovations and diminishing GHG outflows. Governments can utilize a range of policy instruments, such as carbon estimating, regulations, endowments, and public ventures, to advance the move to low-carbon economies. For example, carbon estimating policies, such as carbon charges and outflows exchanging plans, can create motivations for businesses and individuals to decrease their GHG emanations. Regulations can also be utilized to promote the adoption of energy-efficient technologies and renewable energy sources.

International cooperation is fundamental in addressing climate change, because it requires collective action from all nations. International cooperation can take numerous forms, such as knowledge-sharing, innovation exchange, capacity-building, and budgetary support. Developed nations have a obligation to support developing nations in their efforts to moderate and adapt to climate change, as they have verifiably contributed more to GHG emissions and have more prominent financial and technical resources.

The United Nations Framework Convention on Climate Change (UNFCCC) is the primary international treaty administering global endeavors to combat climate change. The UNFCCC provides a system for international cooperation on climate change, including the adoption of the Paris Agreement. The UNFCCC moreover organizes annual Conferences of the Parties (COP) to review and assess advance on global efforts to combat climate change.

One of the basic issues in international climate negotiations is the principle of common but differentiated responsibilities and respective capabilities (CBDR-RC). The CBDR-RC guideline recognizes that developed nations have a historical obligation for climate change and have greater financial and technical resources to address it. Developing countries have a right to advancement and require support from developed nations to mitigate and adapt to climate change.

International climate finance is a significant component of international cooperation, as it gives budgetary support to developing nations to mitigate and adapt to climate change. Developed nations have committed to giving $100 billion per year in climate finance to developing nations by 2020, with a objective of expanding the amount of climate finance in the future. Climate finance can take numerous forms, such as grants, loans, and investments in renewable energy and energy efficiency ventures.

Innovation exchange is another basic component of international cooperation on climate change. Developing nations require access to low-carbon innovations to decrease their GHG outflows and advance sustainable advancement. Developed nations have a responsibility to support technology transfer to developing nations through different components, such as capacity-building, technical help, and financial support.

In conclusion, policy and international cooperation play a crucial role in mitigating climate change by diminishing GHG emanations and advancing sustainable development. The Paris Agreement gives a framework for international cooperation on climate change, and policies can be utilized to advance the adoption of low-carbon innovations. Developed nations have a obligation to support developing nations in their efforts to moderate and adapt to climate change, including through international climate finance and innovation transfer.

In order to mitigate climate change by diminishing greenhouse gas (GHG) outflows and advancing sustainable advancement, collective action from individuals, the private sector, and governments is fundamental. we'll conversation almost how each industry contributes to achieving these targets and how they can collaborate to create the future more sustainable.

By establishing policies, regulations, and guidelines that empower sustainable development and diminish greenhouse gas (GHG) emissions, governments play a vital role in climate change mitigation. Policies like carbon estimating, mandates for renewable energy, energy efficiency measures, and regulations on vehicle and industry outflows can be executed by governments. Low-carbon innovation advancement and greenhouse gas emanations can both advantage from these policies.

By 2030, the European Union (EU) intends to cut greenhouse gas (GHG) emanations by 55% compared to 1990 levels. The EU has implemented approaches just like the EU Emissions Trading System, which permits power plants and industries to exchange emissions allowances and imposes a cap on their emanations. The European Union has also set a goal of having 32% of its energy blend come from renewable sources by 2030.

By contributing in naturally inviting infrastructure like renewable energy, energy-efficient buildings, and public transportation, governments can also support sustainable development. As a result, GHG emanations can be reduced, new job opportunities can be created, and financial development can be fed.

The confidential range likewise assumes a urgent part in soothing natural change by putting resources into low-carbon propels, progressing reasonable hones, and diminishing their carbon impression. To reduce their impact on the environment, private businesses can make speculations in sustainable production methods, energy-efficient innovations, and renewable energy. Google, for instance, has committed to running its business totally on renewable energy and has invested in large-scale renewable energy ventures like wind and solar ranches.

In addition, the private sector can contribute to the cause of economical advancement by consolidating sustainability into their supply chains and business strategies. Maintainability measures can be set up by businesses for their suppliers and they can work with them to diminish their carbon footprint. This could assist with making a more economical store network and development maintainable turn of occasions.

By pushing for change and embracing feasible lifestyle choices, individuals also play a pivotal role in reducing the impacts of climate change. Individuals can lessen their carbon impression by utilizing public transportation, diminishing their energy utilization, and going with reasonable food choices. In addition, people can contact their elected officials, sign petitions, and participate in challenges to advocate for change.

For instance, the Fridays for Future movement, which Greta Thunberg started, has assembled millions of people all over the world to contradict climate change and call on their governments to take action. This movement has pushed governments to take action and helped raise awareness of climate change.

A more effective and long-lasting methodology for mitigating climate change can be developed through collective action from all three sectors. The private sector can contribute in low-carbon innovations and advance sustainable practices, people can make sustainable lifestyle choices and advocate for change, and governments can provide the fundamental policies and regulations to advance sustainable improvement.

Furthermore, sector-to-sector collaboration can speed up the transition to a sustainable future and help in the creation of new opportunities. Incentives for the private division to contribute in low-carbon innovations and advance maintainable hones. People can also play a noteworthy role in moderating climate change by embracing economical practices in their daily lives. The private segment and governments can collaborate to create policies that promote economic improvement and decrease GHG emanations. Utilizing public transportation, cycling or strolling instead of driving, consuming a plant-based diet, reducing food waste, and decreasing energy utilization at domestic are all ways individuals can diminish their carbon impression. By taking on conservative practices in their regular schedules, individuals can add to the aggregate work to reduce GHG releases and fight environmental change.

Chapter 6

Climate Policies and Regulations

Agreements and Treaties on Climate Change

Climate change could be a worldwide issue that requires a facilitated response from governments, organizations, and people around the world. In recent decades, various agreements and treaties have been signed to address the issue of climate change and decrease greenhouse gas outflows. These agreements represent a critical step towards a more sustainable future, but there are still many challenges that must be overcome.

The first international agreement on climate change was the United Nations Framework Convention on Climate Change (UNFCCC), signed in 1992. The UNFCCC is a legally binding treaty that aims to stabilize greenhouse gas concentrations in the atmosphere and avoid dangerous anthropogenic impedances with the climate framework. It sets out a system for international cooperation on climate change, including the guideline of "common but differentiated responsibilities," which recognizes that developed nations have a greater responsibility to diminish emanations than developing nations. The UNFCCC has been approved by 197 countries, including the United States, and serves as the foundation for ensuing climate change agreements (United Nations Framework Convention on Climate Change).

The most noteworthy agreement to emerge from the UNFCCC was the Kyoto Protocol, signed in 1997. The Kyoto Protocol was the first worldwide treaty to establish legitimately binding emissions reduction targets for developed countries. It required signatories to reduce their greenhouse gas emanations by an average of 5.2% below 1990 levels by 2012. The Kyoto Protocol was significant because it represented a collective commitment to reducing emanations and provided a framework for international cooperation on climate change. However, the

Kyoto Protocol had a few impediments, including the fact that it did not incorporate emanations reduction targets for developing countries, which were rapidly industrializing and contributing to the issue of climate change. Moreover, the United States, the world's largest emitter of greenhouse gasses at the time, did not approve the Kyoto Protocol (United Nations Framework Convention on Climate Change).

In 2015, the Paris Agreement was signed, representing a significant step forward in the global exertion to address climate change. The Paris Agreement is a legally authoritative treaty that aims to constrain global warming to well below 2 degrees Celsius above pre-industrial levels and seek after endeavors to constrain it to 1.5 degrees Celsius. The Paris Agreement requires signatories to submit nationally determined contributions (NDCs) outlining their emanations reduction targets and efforts to adapt to the impacts of climate change. The Paris Agreement also includes provisions for financing, innovation exchange, and capacity building to support developing countries in their endeavors to address climate change. As of 2021, 191 nations have approved the Paris Agreement, including the United States, which rejoined the agreement under the Biden administration (United Nations Framework Convention on Climate Change).

While the Paris Agreement represents a significant step forward in the worldwide effort to address climate change, there are still numerous challenges that must be overcome. One of the biggest challenges is the require for more prominent aspiration in outflows reduction targets. The current NDCs submitted by signatories are not adequate to meet the objectives of the Paris Agreement, and there is a need for more forceful emissions reduction targets to restrain global warming to 1.5 degrees Celsius. Also, there is a need for increased financing and support for developing countries to offer assistance them move to low-carbon economies and adjust to the impacts of climate change (United Nations Framework Convention on Climate Change).

National Climate Policies and Regulations

National climate policies and regulations play a pivotal role in moderating greenhouse gas emanations and addressing climate change at a local level. This part of the chapter will give an outline of the significance of national climate policies and regulations and explore some of the most effective approaches to handling climate change at the national level.

National climate policies and regulations are fundamental for addressing climate change because they empower nations to take particular actions to diminish their greenhouse gas emissions and adapt to the impacts of climate change. These policies and regulations provide a framework for action and facilitate the coordination of efforts between diverse levels of government and across different sectors of the economy. National climate policies and regulations can help to mobilize public and private investment in low-carbon innovations and encourage development in the advancement of new, sustainable products and services (World Resources Institute)

One of the most effective approaches to reducing greenhouse gas emanations at the national level is the implementation of a carbon estimating mechanism. A carbon estimating mechanism can take the form of a carbon charge or a cap-and-trade system, both of which aim to put a price on carbon emanations and provide an economic incentive for companies and people to reduce their carbon impression. Carbon estimating mechanisms have been executed in several nations, including Sweden, Norway, and Canada, and have been shown to be effective in decreasing emanations while generating revenue that can be reinvested in climate mitigation and adaptation measures (World Bank, 2021).

In addition to carbon estimating mechanisms, national climate policies and regulations can also incorporate renewable energy targets, energy efficiency guidelines, and regulations on outflows from transportation and industry. Renewable energy targets aim to increase the share of renewable energy sources in a country's energy mix, while energy efficiency standards require buildings and appliances to meet minimum energy efficiency standards. Regulations on emissions from transportation and industry can incorporate fuel economy benchmarks for vehicles, emissions limits for power plants, and regulations on industrial processes that emit greenhouse gases (World Resources Institute).

One of the most significant national climate policies is the European Union Emissions Trading System (EU ETS), which was propelled in 2005. The EU ETS is the biggest outflows trading system in the world and covers more than 11,000 industrial and power plants in 31 countries. The system aims to diminish greenhouse gas emanations by requiring companies to buy grants to emit carbon dioxide and other gases. The number of grants accessible is constrained, and the cap diminishes each year, leading to a reduction in emissions over time. The EU ETS has been successful in reducing emissions in the industries it covers, and the system is being expanded to include more sectors, such as aviation (European Commission, 2021).

In the United States, the Clean Air Act is the primary national policy for reducing greenhouse gas emanations. The Clean Air Act was first passed in 1963 and has been amended several times since then to incorporate provisions for addressing climate change. Under the Clean Air Act, the Environmental Protection Agency (EPA) is responsible for controlling greenhouse gas emanations from expansive sources such as power plants, refineries, and industrial facilities. The EPA has also established fuel efficiency standards for vehicles and equipment, which have helped to decrease emissions from the transportation sector (Environmental Protection Agency).

Another vital national climate policy is China's National Plan on Climate Change (NPCC), which was first introduced in 2007. The NPCC sets out a extend of measures to reduce greenhouse gas emissions, including increasing the utilize of renewable energy sources, improving energy efficiency, and promoting the development of low-carbon industries. China is the world's largest emitter of greenhouse gases, and the NPCC represents a significant commitment to addressing climate change. In recent years, China has made significant progress in reducing its emissions, and the country is now a global pioneer in renewable energy investment and deployment (National Development and Reform Commission, 2019).

One example of a country with a comprehensive set of national climate policies and regulations is Denmark. Denmark has set driven targets for reducing greenhouse gas emissions and expanding the share of renewable energy in its energy blend. The nation has actualized a carbon estimating mechanism in the form of a carbon assessment and has also set energy efficiency standards for buildings and appliances. Moreover, Denmark has implemented regulations on emissions from transportation and industry, including an objective of phasing out the deal of new gasoline and diesel cars by 2030 (Government of Denmark).

Another example of effective national climate policies and regulations can be found in Costa Rica. Costa Rica has set an objective of becoming carbon neutral by 2050 and has implemented several policies to achieve this objective. The nation has executed a carbon charge and has set renewable energy targets, with the objective of generating 100% of its electricity from renewable sources by 2030. Costa Rica has also executed regulations on emissions from transportation and industry, including fuel economy guidelines for vehicles and emissions limits for power plants (Government of Costa Rica).

While national climate policies and regulations have been effective in reducing greenhouse gas emanations and addressing the impacts of climate change in numerous nations, there are still many challenges that must be overcome. One of the greatest challenges is the need for greater desire in emanations reduction targets. Many countries have set targets that are not sufficient to meet the goals of international agreements such as the Paris Agreement. Also, there's a need for expanded financing and support for developing countries to assist them transition to low-carbon economies and adapt to the impacts of climate change (United Nations Framework Convention on Climate Change).

National climate policies and regulations play a critical role in addressing climate change at a local level. These policies and regulations provide a system for action and facilitate the coordination of efforts between distinctive levels of government and across different sectors of the economy.

Climate Initiatives at the Local and Regional Levels

National climate policies and regulations play a pivotal role in moderating greenhouse gas emanations and addressing climate change at a local level. This part of the chapter will give an outline of the significance of national climate policies and regulations and explore some of the most effective approaches to handling climate change at the national level.

National climate policies and regulations are fundamental for addressing climate change because they empower nations to take particular actions to diminish their greenhouse gas emissions and adapt to the impacts of climate change. These policies and regulations provide a framework for action and facilitate the coordination of efforts between diverse levels of government and across different sectors of the economy. National climate policies and regulations can help to mobilize public and private investment in low-carbon innovations and encourage development in the advancement of new, sustainable products and services (World Resources Institute)

One of the most effective approaches to reducing greenhouse gas emanations at the national level is the implementation of a carbon estimating mechanism. A carbon estimating mechanism can take the form of a carbon charge or a cap-and-trade system, both of which aim to put a price on carbon emanations and provide an economic incentive for companies and people to reduce their carbon impression. Carbon estimating mechanisms have been executed in several nations, including Sweden, Norway, and Canada, and have been shown to be effective in decreasing emanations while generating revenue that can be reinvested in climate mitigation and adaptation measures (World Bank, 2021).

In addition to carbon estimating mechanisms, national climate policies and regulations can also incorporate renewable energy targets, energy efficiency guidelines, and regulations on outflows from transportation and industry. Renewable energy targets aim to increase the share of renewable energy sources in a country's energy mix, while energy efficiency standards require buildings and appliances to meet minimum energy efficiency standards. Regulations on emissions from transportation and industry can incorporate fuel economy benchmarks for vehicles, emissions limits for power plants, and regulations on industrial processes that emit greenhouse gases (World Resources Institute).

One of the most significant national climate policies is the European Union Emissions Trading System (EU ETS), which was propelled in 2005. The EU ETS is the biggest outflows trading system in the world and covers more than 11,000 industrial and power plants in 31 countries. The system aims to diminish greenhouse gas emanations by requiring companies to buy grants to emit carbon dioxide and other gases. The number of grants accessible is constrained, and the cap diminishes each year, leading to a reduction in emissions over time. The EU ETS has been successful in reducing emissions in the industries it covers, and the system is being expanded to include more sectors, such as aviation (European Commission, 2021).

In the United States, the Clean Air Act is the primary national policy for reducing greenhouse gas emanations. The Clean Air Act was first passed in 1963 and has been amended several times since then to incorporate provisions for addressing climate change. Under the Clean Air Act, the Environmental Protection Agency (EPA) is responsible for controlling greenhouse gas emanations from expansive sources such as power plants, refineries, and industrial facilities. The EPA has also established fuel efficiency standards for vehicles and equipment, which have helped to decrease emissions from the transportation sector (Environmental Protection Agency).

Another vital national climate policy is China's National Plan on Climate Change (NPCC), which was first introduced in 2007. The NPCC sets out a extend of measures to reduce greenhouse gas emissions, including increasing the utilize of renewable energy sources, improving energy efficiency, and promoting the development of low-carbon industries. China is the world's largest emitter of greenhouse gases, and the NPCC represents a significant commitment to addressing climate change. In recent years, China has made significant progress in reducing its emissions, and the country is now a global pioneer in renewable energy investment and deployment (National Development and Reform Commission, 2019).

One example of a country with a comprehensive set of national climate policies and regulations is Denmark. Denmark has set driven targets for reducing greenhouse gas emissions and expanding the share of renewable energy in its energy blend. The nation has actualized a carbon estimating mechanism in the form of a carbon assess, and has also set energy efficiency standards for buildings and appliances. Moreover, Denmark has implemented regulations on emissions from transportation and industry, including a objective of phasing out the deal of new gasoline and diesel cars by 2030 (Government of Denmark).

Another example of effective national climate policies and regulations can be found in Costa Rica. Costa Rica has set a objective of becoming carbon neutral by 2050 and has implemented several policies to achieve this objective. The nation has executed a carbon charge and has set renewable energy targets, with a objective of generating 100% of its electricity from renewable sources by 2030. Costa Rica has also executed regulations on emissions from transportation and industry, including fuel economy guidelines for vehicles and emissions limits for power plants (Government of Costa Rica).

While national climate policies and regulations have been effective in reducing greenhouse gas emanations and addressing the impacts of climate change in numerous nations, there are still many challenges that must be overcome. One of the greatest challenges is the need for greater desire in emanations reduction targets. Many countries have set targets that are not sufficient to meet the goals of international agreements such as the Paris Agreement. Also, there's a need for expanded financing and support for developing countries to assist them transition to low-carbon economies and adapt to the impacts of climate change (United Nations Framework Convention on Climate Change).

National climate policies and regulations play a critical role in addressing climate change at a local level. These policies and regulations provide a system for action and facilitate the coordination of efforts between distinctive levels of government and across different sectors of the economy.

Taking Climate Action Through Market Mechanisms

Market mechanisms, such as carbon markets, are complementary measures that help accomplish climate change mitigation targets at the lowest possible cost (IISD 2021). Carbon markets incentivize climate action by empowering parties to trade carbon credits generated by the reduction or removal of GHGs from the atmosphere (The World Bank 2022). Article 6 of the Paris Agreement provides a framework for trading GHG emission reductions between countries under the supervision of the Conference of Parties (United Nations Climate Change 2023). The Article 6.4 mechanism enables the trading of emission reduction and removal credits generated through specific activities implemented in participating countries (UNFCCC 2023). Article 6.8 recognizes non-market approaches to promote mitigation and adaptation (The World Bank 2022). The text of Article 6.4(b) of the Paris Agreement provides for "participation in the mitigation of greenhouse gas emissions by public and private entities.

Taking climate action through market mechanisms includes using economic incentives and market-based solutions to reduce greenhouse gas emanations and promote sustainable practices. These mechanisms can take many shapes, including carbon estimating, emanations exchange, and clean energy endowments. In recent years, market mechanisms have gained notoriety as a implies of addressing climate change, particularly in countries that have struggled to execute traditional regulatory approaches. We will explore some of the foremost common market mechanisms used to tackle climate change and their effectiveness in promoting sustainable development.

One of the foremost popular market mechanisms for reducing greenhouse gas emanations is carbon pricing. Carbon pricing involves placing a price on carbon emissions through an assessment or cap-and-trade framework. A carbon assessment includes placing a direct assessment on carbon emissions, whereas a cap-and-trade framework sets a restrain on emanations and permits companies to trade emissions allowances. Carbon pricing has been actualized in many countries around the world, including the European Union, Canada, and China. Studies have shown that carbon pricing can successfully diminish greenhouse gas emissions and empower the adoption of clean energy innovations (Stavins, 2019). However, carbon pricing can also be backward, meaning that it can excessively affect low-income families. It is important to guarantee that any carbon pricing system incorporates measures to protect vulnerable populations and promote a just transition to a low-carbon economy.

Another market mechanism used to handle climate change is emanations trading. Emanations trading allows companies to trade emanations allowances, making a market for emissions reductions. Companies that emanate less than their allowance can offer their surplus allowances to those that exceed their allowance. The objective of emissions trading is to create a financial incentive for companies to decrease their emissions and invest in clean energy innovations. Emanations trading has been effectively executed in the European Union, where it has contributed to a significant reduction in greenhouse gas emissions. However, the effectiveness of emanations trading can depend on the design of the system, including the initial allocation of allowances and the use of offsets.

Governments can also use subsidies and incentives to promote clean energy and sustainable practices. Clean energy subsidies can incorporate direct subsidies for renewable energy projects, tax credits for clean energy investments, and feed-in taxes for renewable energy generation. These subsidies can help to form clean energy technologies more reasonable and competitive with fossil fuels. Incentives can also be used to promote sustainable practices, such as building codes that require energy-efficient buildings or transportation policies that encourage the use of public transit. In any case, subsidies and incentives can be expensive and can mutilate the market, so it is vital to carefully design and execute them to ensure their effectiveness and efficiency.

Other market mechanisms that can be used to address climate change incorporate emissions trading, renewable energy certificates (RECs), and deliberate carbon offsets. Emanations trading, also known as cap-and-trade, is a framework in which a cap is set on the total amount of greenhouse gas emanations that can be released by a group of emitters. The emitters are then allocated permits to emanate a certain amount of greenhouse gases, which they can trade among themselves. This creates a market for emissions reductions, as emitters who can reduce their emissions more cheaply can sell their grants to those who cannot. This incentivizes emissions reductions in the most cost-effective way possible. The European Union Emissions Trading System (EU ETS) is the world's biggest emissions trading scheme, covering over 11,000 power plants and industrial facilities (European Commission, 2020).

RECs are certificates that represent the environmental attributes of one megawatt-hour (MWh) of power generated from a renewable source. They can be bought and sold separately from the power itself, permitting people and organizations to support renewable energy development without having to physically purchase renewable power. RECs are commonly used by companies to meet their sustainability goals and support the development of renewable energy. The Renewable Energy Certificate System (RECS) is an international system for tracking and trading RECs (International REC Standard).

Voluntary carbon offsets are credits that represent a reduction in greenhouse gas emissions outside of the emitter's direct control. People and organizations can purchase carbon offsets to compensate for their own emissions, effectively neutralizing their carbon footprint. Carbon offsets are regularly generated from projects such as reforestation, renewable energy development, and energy efficiency improvements.

While market mechanisms can be effective tools for addressing climate change, there are also some impediments to their use. One impediment is that they may not be sufficient to address some of the more complex and systemic challenges of climate change, such as the need to shift away from fossil fuels and towards renewable energy sources. Market mechanisms may also be more effective in some contexts than in others, depending on factors such as political will, economic conditions, and the nature of the environmental challenges being addressed (Jagers & Stripple, 2021).

Though the market mechanisms have the potential to reduce greenhouse gas emissions in a cost-effective manner, they are not without challenges. One of the biggest challenges is ensuring that the market is transparent and free from fraud, which can undermine the integrity of the system. Another challenge is ensuring that the benefits of emissions reductions are distributed reasonably and do not excessively harm vulnerable communities. Also, market mechanisms are not a substitute for government regulation and policy, as they do not address other important social and environmental goals beyond reducing greenhouse gas emissions (World Resources Institute, 2021). It is important to recognize the limitations of market mechanisms and to ensure that they are part of a broader suite of policy measures aimed at promoting sustainable development.

Market mechanisms can play an important role in diminishing greenhouse gas emissions and addressing climate change. However, they are not without challenges and must be implemented in a transparent and reasonable way. Market mechanisms should be viewed as complementary to government policy and regulation, rather than a substitute.

Government's Role in Addressing Climate Change

Governments play a pivotal role in addressing climate change by creating policies, and regulations, funding research, and developing of new advances to reduce greenhouse gas emissions. The role of governments in addressing climate change varies significantly depending on their political, economic, and social contexts.

Governments can confront climate change in a few ways. One way is to protect and restore key ecosystems such as rivers, wetlands, oceans, forests, and mangroves that absorb large quantities of carbon, slowing warming (AIDA-Americans 2017). Governments can also support small agricultural producers and promote clean energy (AIDA-Americans 2017). Another way is to pressure governments and businesses to keep fossil fuels in the ground and move their economies away from fossil fuels as soon as possible (Greenpeace). Individuals can also play a part by making better choices about where they get their energy, how they travel, and what food they eat. However, the most ideal way for anyone to help stop climate change is to take collective action by pressuring governments and corporations to change their policies and business practices.

The government of Sweden has been recognized as a global pioneer in climate action, having set a target of accomplishing net-zero greenhouse gas emissions by 2045. Sweden has implemented a range of measures to diminish emissions, including a carbon assess, subsidies for electric vehicles, and investments in renewable energy. The government has also committed to increasing the use of public transportation and reducing the use of fossil fuels in the transportation sector. Sweden's ambitious climate policies have earned it recognition as a global leader in climate action (Dagens Nyheter, 2022).

Germany has been implementing a extend of policies to address climate change, including a feed-in tariff system to promote the use of renewable energy, regulations on energy efficiency in buildings, and a tax on carbon emissions. The country has set a target of reducing its greenhouse gas emissions by at least 55% by 2030 compared to 1990 levels. Germany's policies have been successful in reducing greenhouse gas emissions, and the country has been able to maintain a strong economy while transitioning to a low-carbon future (Clean Energy Wire, 2021).

In contrast, a few governments have been criticized for their lack of action on climate change. For example, the government of the United States under the Trump administration withdrew from the Paris Agreement, a global effort to combat climate change. However, the Biden administration has taken steps to reduce greenhouse gas emissions, including rejoining the Paris Climate Agreement, committing to a goal of net-zero emissions by 2050, and investing in renewable energy. The US government's role in addressing climate change has been hindered by political polarization and opposition from the fossil fuel industry (The New York Times, 2021).

The government of Australia has been criticized for its need of action on climate change, despite being one of the countries most affected by it. The country has been experiencing more frequent and severe heatwaves, droughts, and bushfires in recent years, and experts predict that these events will continue to worsen unless emissions are reduced. However, the Australian government has been slow to implement policies to address climate change and has even continued to support the coal industry, one of the biggest contributors to greenhouse gas emissions (Johnston, I. (2019, January 7).

Besides, the government of India has been criticized for its lack of action on climate change, despite being the third-largest emitter of greenhouse gases. Although the Indian government has set targets for increasing the use of renewable energy, it has also continued to support the use of coal and other fossil fuels. Moreover, the country has been moderate to actualize policies to diminish emanations within the transportation division, which is a major contributor to greenhouse gas outflows. The Indian government has faced challenges in implementing policies to address climate change, including political opposition and the need to adjust economic growth with natural protection (Government of India. (2021).

China, as the world's largest emitter of greenhouse gases, has recently taken steps to address climate change. The government has set a target of achieving peak carbon emissions by 2030 and carbon neutrality by 2060. To achieve these targets, the government has implemented policies to increase the use of renewable energy, phase out coal-fired power plants, and promote electric vehicles. China's efforts to address climate change are critical to the success of global efforts to combat climate change, given the country's significant contribution to greenhouse gas emissions (BBC News, 2021).

Other countries, such as Denmark, have also implemented ambitious climate policies. Denmark aims to reduce its greenhouse gas emissions by 70% by 2030 compared to 1990 levels, and it has implemented a range of measures to achieve this target, including investments in wind energy and energy-efficient buildings (Energy Watch Group, 2021). The Netherlands has set a target of reducing greenhouse gas emissions by 49%by 2030 compared to 1990 levels and has implemented a range of measures to achieve this target, including regulations on energy efficiency in buildings and the promotion of electric vehicles (Government of the Netherlands, 2021).

The government of Norway has been at the forefront of the global battle against climate change. The country has set a goal of becoming climate neutral by 2030, and has executed a range of measures to reduce outflows, including a carbon tax, investments in renewable energy, and a cap-and-trade system. Moreover, the Norwegian government has launched several initiatives to reduce emissions in the transportation sector, such as incentives for electric vehicles, low-emission zones, and investment in sustainable public transportation. These initiatives have been successful in reducing greenhouse gas emissions and have earned Norway recognition as a global pioneer in climate action (Government of Norway. (2021).

Similarly, the government of Denmark has implemented a range of policies to address climate change, including a carbon tax, feed-in tariffs for renewable energy, and a target of phasing out fossil fuel use by 2050. Denmark has also invested in wind energy, and currently produces over 40% of its electricity from wind power. Moreover, the government has launched several initiatives to reduce emissions in the transportation sector, such as subsidies for electric vehicles and investment in public transportation. These initiatives have been successful in reducing greenhouse gas outflows, and Denmark has been able to maintain a strong economy whereas transitioning to a low-carbon future (Government of Denmark. (2021).

The government of the United Kingdom has executed a range of policies to address climate change, including a carbon tax, a target of achieving net-zero emissions by 2050, and investments in renewable energy. Besides, the government has launched several initiatives to reduce emissions in the transportation sector, such as subsidies for electric vehicles, investment in public transportation, and a ban on the sale of new petrol and diesel cars from 2030. These initiatives have been effective in reducing greenhouse gas emissions, and the UK has been recognized as a global leader in climate action (Government of the United Kingdom. (2021).

Developing countries, such as Costa Rica, have also implemented innovative climate policies. Costa Rica aims to achieve net-zero greenhouse gas emissions by 2050 and has implemented policies to promote reforestation and the use of renewable energy (Carbon Brief, 2021). Rwanda aims to become a carbon-neutral country by 2050 and has implemented policies to advance renewable energy and decrease deforestation (World Bank, 2021).

There are a number of procedures that governments can use to combat climate change. These procedures incorporate enacting adaptation policies with the goal of making cities, states, and even nations less susceptible to extreme weather events (World101), n.d.)and employing market-based procedures like cap-and-trade policies and clean energy standards. Moreover, governments have the ability to support small agricultural producers, support public transportation, protect and restore important ecosystems, and invest in renewable energy (AIDA-Americans). Since more than 85% of global climate contamination originates outside of the United States (Whitehouse), it is critical that governments collaborate to combat climate change.

Chapter 7

Adapting to Climate Change

The Requirement for Adaptation Strategies in a Changing Climate

Climate change is a pressing problem that has a global impact. This has resulted in a number of outcomes including an increase in ocean levels, a higher occurrence and increased intensity of environmental calamities, and alterations in weather trends. The alterations carry substantial consequences for the environment, financial systems, and employment prospects for people. Hence, it is crucial to implement adaptation measures that help in dealing with the consequences of climate change. (IPCC, 2014)

The processes of adaptation refer to measures implemented in order to deal with or minimize the hazards connected with the effects of climate change. These methods are designed to improve the adaptability of societies, financial systems, and natural environments to cope with the transformations resulting from climate change (UNFCCC, 2015). They have the ability to be put into action at varying degrees, including an individual, community, regional, or national level, based on the situation.

Agricultural workers can adapt to shifting weather patterns and uphold food security by implementing climate-smart farming practices, as outlined by FAO in 2013. In metropolitan areas, cities have the option of implementing tactics like constructing coastal barriers or resettling at-risk communities to address the issue of elevated sea levels (UN-Habitat, 2010). Companies can adopt sustainable measures in the business industry to decrease their ecological impact and enhance their resistance to climate-related hazards (WBCSD, 2020).

The significance of adaptation measures lies in the fact that despite considerable attempts to mitigate it, climate change is predicted to persist (IPCC, 2018). Consequently, appropriate adaptation measures will be crucial in mitigating the effects of climate change on ecosystems, economies, and communities. Effective adaptation procedures demand the cooperation of various factors such as governments, corporations, and societies, as emphasized by the IPCC (2014).

When devising adaptation protocols, it is imperative to take into account the changing effects of climate change on varied regions and communities. The IPCC (2014) suggests that specific areas may have varying levels of susceptibility to either abrupt occurrences like hurricanes and floods or gradual alterations in the environment like shifts in precipitation and temperature patterns. Hence, customization of adaptation strategies based on the unique requirements and attributes of each locality is crucial for achieving desirable outcomes.

A crucial factor to bear in mind is the possible compromises that may arise between endeavors aimed at adaptation and those oriented towards mitigation. Mentioned are certain measures to counteract climate change, where certain mitigation methods, like carbon capture and storage, could potentially harm the biodiversity, while certain adaptation techniques, such as constructing seawalls, may bring changes in the coastal ecosystems. Hence, it is crucial to evaluate the potential advantages and disadvantages of various methodologies with great care.

The successful incorporation of adaptation measures necessitates efficient management and regulatory structures as well. Collaboration between various entities including governments is crucial in establishing and executing measures that facilitate the integration of adaptability protocols (UNFCCC, 2015). To encourage adaptation efforts, various measures such as financial assistance, incentives, or regulatory structures may be introduced. To ensure long-term effectiveness and sustainability, it is imperative that adaptation measures are incorporated into wider development planning and decision-making processes (UN-Habitat, 2010).

Ultimately, the effectiveness of adaptation methods relies on the active participation and investment of both community members and other parties with a stake in the matter. To ensure successful adaptation measures, it is crucial to involve the individuals who are most impacted by climate change, particularly those who are marginalized and vulnerable, according to the IPCC's 2014 report. It is crucial to engage communities in the process of developing, executing, and overseeing adaptation measures so that these strategies meet their specific requirements and address their anxieties.

To successfully adjust to climate change, it is essential to assess the hazards associated with it and take prompt actions to mitigate those risks. Governments and organizations are devising strategies to adapt to the potential climate-related risks affecting various areas of concern. It is important to customize them according to the distinct demands and traits of every area, and deliberate evaluation should be made regarding probable compromises and advantages along with mitigation endeavors. The implementation and success of efficient governance and policy frameworks require crucial factors such as community involvement.

Paradigms of Successful Adaptation Measures

Adaptation is a fundamental process that people, communities, and societies undertake to manage with changes and challenges in their environment. Effective adaptation measures depend on several factors, including the ability to identify and respond to changes, the availability of resources and infrastructure, and social, economic, and political factors. Different paradigms have emerged to guide the development of successful adaptation measures.

One paradigm is the resilience approach, which emphasizes the ability of systems to absorb shocks and maintain their essential functions. This approach acknowledges that changes and challenges are inevitable and encourages building adaptive capacity to mitigate the impacts of these changes. For example, in the context of climate change, communities may develop resilient infrastructure and diversify their jobs to cope with extreme climate events (Pelling, 2011).

Another paradigm is the vulnerability approach, which focuses on the social, economic, and political factors that create vulnerability to changes and challenges. This approach recognizes that some people and communities are more susceptible to the impacts of changes due to factors such as poverty, inequality, and marginalization. Successful adaptation measures using this approach involve addressing the root causes of vulnerability and ensuring that adaptation measures are equitable and inclusive (Adger et al., 2003).

A third paradigm is the adaptive management approach, which emphasizes the iterative and flexible nature of the adaptation. This approach recognizes that the effectiveness of adaptation measures may be uncertain and that learning and adaptation are continuous processes. Fruitful adaptation measures utilizing this approach include monitoring and evaluation to inform future adaptation efforts and building institutional capacity for adaptive management (Folke et al., 2005).

One important factor is the involvement and participation of stakeholders in the adaptation process. Stakeholders can include individuals, groups, organizations, and communities that are affected by changes and challenges in their environment. Engaging stakeholders in the development of adaptation measures can increase their ownership and buy-in and ensure that adaptation measures are tailored to their needs and priorities (Reed et al., 2010).

Another factor is the importance of considering multiple stressors when developing adaptation measures. Changes and challenges in the environment often occur simultaneously, and adaptation measures should account for these interactions. For example, in the context of coastal communities, adaptation measures may need to consider both sea-level rise and storm surge (IPCC, 2019).

The success of adaptation measures can depend on the availability and accessibility of information and knowledge. Adaptation measures often require information about the impacts of changes and potential solutions. Making information available and accessible can improve decision-making and increase the effectiveness of adaptation measures (Smit & Wandel, 2006).

In practice, successful adaptation measures may incorporate elements of multiple paradigms and factors. For example, a successful adaptation measure in a coastal community may involve building resilient infrastructure that can withstand storm surge, engaging stakeholders in the decision-making process, addressing root causes of vulnerability, and monitoring and evaluating the effectiveness of the infrastructure over time.

Overall, successful adaptation measures require a holistic and integrated approach that considers the unique context and characteristics of each system. By consolidating multiple paradigms and factors, and involving stakeholders and considering different stressors, adaptation measures can increase the flexibility and sustainability of people, communities, and societies.

The Role of Ecosystem-Based Approaches to Adaptation

Ecosystem-based approaches to adaptation (EbA) are gaining popularity as a way to increase the resilience of communities to climate change impacts. EbA includes utilizing the administrations provided by natural ecosystems to decrease vulnerability to climate change, such as by preserving wetlands to decrease flood hazard or maintaining healthy forests to prevent landslides. EbA is frequently cost-effective compared to traditional infrastructure-based approaches and can provide extra co-benefits such as biodiversity preservation and improved livelihoods (Barnett & O'Neill, 2010). EbA can moreover provide a more sustainable and long-term solution to climate change adaptation by promoting the preservation and restoration of biological systems, which in turn can improve their ability to provide administrations in the future (IPCC, 2014).

The success of EbA depends on the ability of biological systems to proceed giving the administrations that are required to diminish vulnerability to climate change. This requires the identification and protection of key ecosystems and their administrations, as well as the management of biological system administrations to maintain their functionality (Scherer et al., 2014). In addition, effective administration structures and policies are required to support the implementation of EbA, including ensuring the participation of local communities and stakeholders in decision-making processes (CBD, 2009).

Examples of successful EbA initiatives can be found in various contexts. For instance, in the Philippines, the restoration of mangroves has been appeared to significantly diminish the impact of typhoons and storm surges on coastal communities. In the Peruvian Andes, the restoration of wetlands has helped to decrease the risk of flash floods and landslides caused by extreme rainfall events (Bruijnzeel et al., 2011). In Nepal, the restoration of degraded forests has led to improvements in water quality, reduced erosion and sedimentation, and improved crop yields.

In addition to the examples mentioned above, EbA has also been effectively executed in other contexts. For example, in Kenya, the restoration of degraded land through the planting of indigenous trees and shrubs has appeared to progress soil fertility, increase crop yields, and provide extra benefits such as carbon sequestration and biodiversity preservation. Similarly, in Brazil, the protection and restoration of riparian forests has been effective in reducing the hazard of flooding and erosion, while also giving habitat for endangered species (Ribeiro et al., 2017).

However, the implementation of EbA can also confront challenges, especially in contexts where there's restricted understanding or appreciation of the value of biological system administrations, or where there are competing interests for the utilization of natural resources. For instance, in some areas, the conversion of wetlands to agricultural land has resulted in expanded flood risk and the loss of important biological system administrations, despite the potential benefits of protecting wetlands for flood mitigation. Furthermore, there may be clashes between diverse stakeholders over the utilization of natural resources, such as between preservationists and local communities who depend on forests for their livelihoods.

In general, while EbA has appeared promising as a way to increase the flexibility of communities to climate change impacts, its success depends on effective administration structures, the recognition of the value of biological system administrations, and the involvement of local communities in decision-making processes. By advancing the preservation and restoration of biological systems, EbA can provide a sustainable and long-term solution to climate change adaptation that can also provide additional benefits such as biodiversity conservation and improved livelihoods.

The Importance of Community Engagement in Adaptation Planning

Community engagement is basic for effective climate adaptation planning. Climate change impacts manifest at the community level, and suitable solutions are required to address them; (Susanne Moser, 2015). Community involvement in the planning process makes a difference to ensure effective implementation and progression over electoral cycles. It also helps to ensure that equity goals and processes are explicitly included in the arranging process. Meaningful community engagement involves the direct involvement of those impacted by climate change. It includes various mechanisms for community engagement, such as strong equity-focused committees and the explicit inclusion of equity goals and processes. Agencies must engage with overburdened communities and vulnerable populations when evaluating new and existing programs (Climate Xchange, 2021).

Community engagement is also important in climate-adaptive design projects. The design process is an ideal structure for community participation and problem-solving through experimentation. The design offers powerful tools for deploying interventions with downstream impacts that further marginalize vulnerable communities. It is only when the various components that lend to a community's adaptive capacity are examined, acknowledged, and accounted for that design can be truly equitable (Federal Reserve Bank Of San Francisco,2019). Community engagement platforms can show what climate action implies to communities and help local governments strategize and direct policy interventions to ensure robust and citizen-centric urban planning, solid waste management, transportation, and energy consumption. Locally-led initiatives and community engagement can identify the need for people to transition to a non-carbon future (Hussey, n.d.).

Community engagement in adaptation planning can take many forms. In Florida, community partners and events were used to increase stakeholder participation in adaptation planning projects. The project team also used interviews to create a short film that was posted online and shown at public gatherings to educate the community about the impacts of climate change and to gather feedback on adaptation and community planning (Sherry Spiers et al.).

In San Diego, extensive outreach and engagement was conducted to ensure that the Climate Resilient SD plan spoke to the needs and vision of the city residents. The city used engagement tools to gather feedback on potential draft strategies and refine the selection of adaptation strategies included in the plan (FUTURE). Active engagement can also play a role in evaluating community needs and identifying appropriate solutions. For example, community engagement in climate-adaptive design projects can lift the adaptive capacity of a community.

However, community engagement can be challenging to execute and may require additional government staff and resources. In general, community engagement is critical for successful and comprehensive adaptation planning. It can help guarantee that adaptation planning is meaningful to communities and that their perspectives are incorporated. Community engagement can also help assess community needs, identify appropriate solutions, and increase local capacity to adapt, recover, and flourish amidst a changing climate (Susanne Moser, 2015) .

Whereas community engagement is crucial in adaptation planning, there are also some challenges associated with it. One of the challenges is that community engagement can require additional government staff and significantly protract the project time horizon. Another challenge is that community engagement can be difficult to achieve equitably, as some communities may have more resources and capacity to participate than others (FUTURE). Additionally, community engagement can be challenging when there are conflicting interests or values among stakeholders. It can also be difficult to ensure that the perspectives of all stakeholders are incorporated into the planning process (Kokei Otosi, 2019). Despite these challenges, community engagement is essential in adaptation planning to ensure that adaptation planning is effective and inclusive.

Building Resilience to Climate Change Impacts

Building resilience to climate change impacts involves taking proactive measures to reduce climate risk and accelerate development whereas cutting poverty (The World Bank, 2020). It requires all actors, including governments, communities, and businesses, to have the capacity to anticipate climate dangers and hazards, absorbs shocks and stresses, and reshape and transform development pathways in the longer term (UNFCCC). There are six steps that sectors and actors need to take in developing climate resilience:

1. Awareness-raising and advocacy: Be clear that the future will not resemble the past; base planning on future climate scenarios.
3. Risk assessment: Identify and evaluate climate risks and vulnerabilities.
4. Planning: Develop and implement climate-resilient plans and strategies.
5. Implementation: Implement climate-resilient plans and procedures.
6. Monitoring and evaluation: Monitor and evaluate the effectiveness of climate-resilient plans and strategies.
7. Learning and sharing: Share knowledge and experience to improve climate resilience.

To build resilient foundations with rapid and inclusive development, poverty and the lack of access to basic services, including infrastructure, financial administrations, health care, and social protection, need to be addressed (The World Bank, 2020). Governments will need to manage the risks associated with climate change, including the massive instability that encompasses macroeconomic estimates of future climate change impacts. Businesses take a variety of approaches in addressing risks, including developing disaster recovery plans and adding onsite energy resources (C2ES, n.d.). State governments are crucial in convening local and private interface related to climate change and pooling the resources and expertise of the numerous divisions or agencies that can be influenced by or help address climate change (C2ES, n.d.).

The Building Resilience Against Climate Effects (BRACE) framework is a five-step process that allows health officials to develop strategies and programs to help communities prepare for the health effects of climate change (CDC, 2022). The five steps are:

1. Identify the climate-related health issue.
2. Project the future health impacts.
3. Assess the public health burden.
4. Develop and implement a climate and health adaptation plan.
5. Evaluate the impact of the adaptation plan.

While reducing carbon emissions is essential, effective adaptation to climate change is fundamental to address the increasing frequency of extreme weather events influencing people across the world5. For many developing countries, economic prospects will be significantly threatened without effective adaptation to climate change, and many small island states are particularly vulnerable (IMF, n.d.).

Individual actions that can contribute to building climate resilience include reducing carbon emanations, supporting local and national policies that promote climate resilience, raising awareness around the significance of building climate resilience, and preparing for the impacts of climate change. To reduce carbon emissions, individuals can use public transportation, bike or walk instead of driving, and reduce energy consumption at home. They can also support policies that promote renewable energy and climate adaptation programs.

Raising awareness about the importance of building climate resilience can involve educating others about the impacts of climate change and advocating for action at the community and national levels. Preparing for the impacts of climate change can involve creating emergency kits and developing evacuation plans in case of extreme weather events. Generally, building climate resilience requires action from all actors, including individuals, governments, communities, and businesses (IMF, n.d.) (CDC, 2022).

Preparing for Extreme Weather Events

It is crucial to engage in preparations for severe weather occurrences to minimize harm and guarantee the well-being of both individuals and communities. Adverse weather conditions like hurricanes, tornadoes, floods, and wildfires possess the ability to cause tremendous harm, and they have the potential to emerge unexpectedly. Being prepared, informed, and taking necessary precautions is essential for dealing with such incidents. Having a plan in place is also vital in this regard.

To effectively get ready for harsh weather conditions, it is advisable to possess an emergency kit. The pack ought to include provisions that don't expire easily, clean water, medication, and first-aid essentials, along with vital records such as identification papers and insurance particulars (FEMA, 2022). It is advisable to establish a family communication strategy in the event that family members become separated during the occurrence. (Ready.gov, 2022)

Staying knowledgeable about severe weather conditions is a vital aspect of getting ready for them. Keeping track of weather updates and emergency notifications can supply critical insights into potential dangers and appropriate steps to follow, as recommended by NOAA in 2022. Being knowledgeable about the designated evacuation paths and refuge options is imperative in the event of being required to evacuate (FEMA, 2022).

Implementing vital safety measures can reduce the impact of severe weather besides devising a strategy and staying updated. To safeguard homes from the powerful winds caused by a hurricane or tornado, FEMA suggests taking measures such as fastening outdoor furniture, pruning trees and shrubs, and fortifying windows and doors. Clearing gutters and drains is one way to curb flooding and mitigate any harm that may come to properties and households (Ready. gov, 2022)

There are various alternative methods to prepare for severe weather conditions. It is crucial to comprehend the potential hazards linked to various forms of severe atmospheric phenomena and their potential consequences in your locality. Suppose you're residing in a region prone to wildfires, in that scenario, it's advisable to implement precautionary measures like eliminating excess vegetation and setting up a defensive perimeter around your residence (US Forest Service, 2022). If your residential area is prone to flooding, it may be wise to contemplate buying insurance that safeguards your dwelling against such hazards in order to prevent financial loss (FEMA, 2022).

It is important to take into account the potential consequences on susceptible groups, including but not limited to children, the elderly, and individuals with disabilities, while preparing for severe weather conditions. To guarantee the security and welfare of these communities, it is crucial to establish a strategy that could entail pinpointing convenient havens or means of transportation (Ready. gov, 2022)

It takes collective action to be prepared for severe weather occurrences. Local officials and emergency management teams are highly essential in disseminating crucial information to citizens, such as evacuation directives and the whereabouts of emergency shelters, explained by FEMA (2022). Moreover, residents can aid one another through the exchange of knowledge and supplies, monitoring the well-being of their neighbors, and participating in crisis management initiatives as volunteers (Ready. gov, 2022)

To successfully prepare for extreme weather conditions, one must engage in a comprehensive strategy of planning, remaining updated, and implementing essential safety measures, all of which can help reduce harm and protect the well-being of both individuals and communities. There are various situations that could be considered, such as getting ready for hot temperatures in densely populated regions or bracing for cold snowstorms in less populated regions.

Protecting Vulnerable Populations

Protecting vulnerable populations is a critical aspect of emergency preparedness and response. Vulnerable populations include individuals who may be at higher risk during a disaster, such as children, elderly individuals, individuals with disabilities, pregnant women, and individuals encountering homelessness. It is fundamental to take steps to ensure the safety and well-being of these populations before, during, and after an emergency.

One way to protect vulnerable populations is to create a comprehensive emergency plan that incorporates methodologies for assisting these groups. This plan should include procedures for evacuating, sheltering, and providing medical care and supplies for vulnerable populations (CDC, 2022). It is also important to ensure that emergency shelters are accessible to individuals with disabilities and that they have necessary equipment, such as lifts and ramps (ADA National Network, 2022).

In addition to planning, providing education and resources to vulnerable populations is critical in protecting them during an emergency. This may involve distributing emergency kits that are tailored to their needs, such as medications, assistive devices, and baby supplies (FEMA, 2022). Providing information on how to prepare for an emergency, including evacuation routes and emergency contacts, can also be helpful (Ready.gov, 2022).

During an emergency, it is essential to prioritize the needs of vulnerable populations, including providing access to food, water, and medical care. It is also critical to have a system for identifying and locating people who may need additional assistance, such as those with mobility impairments or language barriers (CDC, 2022).

After an emergency, it is critical to provide support and resources to assist vulnerable populations recover. This may include connecting people with social services and resources, such as disaster relief funds or mental health services (FEMA,

2022). Ensuring that emergency shelters are accessible and have necessary accommodations for people with disabilities is also vital during the recovery period (ADA National Network, 2022).

protecting vulnerable populations is a crucial aspect of emergency preparedness and response. Creating comprehensive emergency plans, providing education and resources, prioritizing their needs during an emergency, and providing support during the recovery period, we can ensure the safety and well-being of vulnerable populations in our communities. Examples of different contexts might incorporate protecting vulnerable populations during extreme weather events, pandemics, or terrorist attacks.

Chapter 8

Effective Actions Should Take

The Need for Urgent and Bold Action to Encounter Climate Change

The pressing issue plaguing humanity these days is undoubtedly climate change, whose effects are being experienced worldwide. Immediate and impactful measures must be taken to address this problem and avert the potential dire outcomes. The IPCC cautioned that if significant measures are not taken to cut down on emissions of greenhouse gases, we may witness a surge in worldwide temperatures by more than 1. 5°C from levels seen in the pre-industrial era by the conclusion of this century. This outcome could have catastrophic effects on both the earth and its living beings.

It is not only a concern for the environment, but also a matter of social justice that calls for immediate and courageous action. Climate change disproportionately impacts the most susceptible societies by worsening disparities and leading to increased destitution, malnutrition, and displacement (IPCC, 2018). In nations where agriculture serves as the primary means of support, such as those in the developing world, the effects of climate change - exemplified by flooding or drought - often result in crop loss, insufficient food supplies, and an increase in malnourishment, according to the Food and Agriculture Organization. Moreover, communities suffer greatly from the consequences of severe weather events like hurricanes, wildfires, and floods, resulting in fatalities, displacement, and financial losses (IPCC, 2018).

Climate change is a worldwide concern that has diverse impacts on every nation. Different countries have varying degrees of susceptibility to the effects of greenhouse gas emissions and diverse levels of responsibility for contributing to these emissions. Swift and daring measures are imperative from every nation to tackle this problem and avert its catastrophic effects.

Small island developing states (SIDS) are particularly susceptible to the consequences of climate change, including occurrences like the rise of sea levels, the acidification of oceans, and extreme weather conditions (UNDESA, 2021), for instance. Tuvalu, a nation located in the Pacific Island region, is facing a severe threat of submergence of its low-lying regions and contamination of its freshwater resources due to the rising sea levels (UNDP, 2021). The Caribbean has been experiencing more frequent and intense hurricanes, leading to notable harm to infrastructure and disrupting tourism, which is a crucial source of revenue for numerous nations in that area (UNEP, 2021). These countries require resolute and effective measures to adjust to the effects of climate change and decrease their susceptibilities.

Conversely, certain countries bear a larger obligation to diminish their release of greenhouse gases. According to the World Resources Institute in 2021, the primary contributors to global greenhouse gas emissions are the United States, China, and the European Union. These nations must promptly and courageously implement measures aimed at minimizing their greenhouse gas emissions and shifting towards economies with reduced carbon footprint. The European Union has established a goal to decrease its emissions by a minimum of 55% by the year 2030 and to reach a state of zero emissions by 2050, according to the European Commission in 2020. China has made a firm pledge to attain its maximum level of emissions by 2030, with an ultimate intention of becoming carbon neutral by 2060 as according to reports by Xinhua in 2020. The White House has announced that the United States has once again become a member of the Paris Agreement and committed to reducing its emissions by 50-52% before the year 2030.

Many developing countries are encountering substantial difficulties in managing their economic growth and lowering their emissions of greenhouse gases. India, ranked as the third largest emitter of greenhouse gases, continues to heavily rely on coal to meet its energy demands according to IEA's 2021 report. India has established formidable objectives to enhance its renewable energy capability and decrease its outflows intensity, as declared by the Indian Government in 2021. Numerous African countries are engaged in a struggle to provide their populations with modern energy services while simultaneously minimizing their emissions, according to IRENA's 2020 report. These countries urgently need daring and proactive measures to shift towards environmentally friendly and low-emission economies while also ensuring that their developmental necessities are fulfilled.

Immediate and daring measures are required at every level, starting from individuals up to enterprises and governments. The IPCC (2018) suggests that one way to mitigate climate change is to shift towards sustainable energy sources, enhance energy efficiency, and allocate resources towards low-carbon infrastructure to decrease greenhouse gas emissions. The statement suggests that we need to modify our consumption habits and minimize waste, alongside allocating resources to climate adaptation initiatives that can aid communities that are at risk to better adapt to the effects of climate change (IPCC, 2018). The implementation of policies that promote sustainable living and the adoption of low-carbon technologies by businesses can be greatly facilitated by the government, directed by the IPCC in 2018.

Swift and daring measures must be taken to tackle the issue of climate change and avert its devastating consequences on both our environment and its inhabitants. Each country needs to consider its specific situation and hurdles and create strategies to decrease the emission of greenhouse gases, adjust to the consequences of climate change, and shift towards sustainable and eco-friendly economies. If immediate action is not taken, the consequences for the planet and future generations will be grave.

The Role of Individuals, Governments, and Corporations in Addressing the Crisis

Currently, one of the most pressing issues facing the human race is the issue of climate change, which has worldwide repercussions. Immediate and attention-grabbing measures must be taken to tackle this problem and avert the possibility of the most disastrous outcomes becoming a fact. According to the IPCC, urgent measures are required to diminish greenhouse gas emissions, or else we may witness a catastrophic increase in global temperatures that exceed pre-industrial levels by 1. 5°C by the close of the century, threatening both the planet and its inhabitants.

Emergent and courageous measures are imperative not only from an environmental perspective but also with regard to the principles of equity and fairness in society. According to the IPCC's 2018 report, climate change disproportionately impacts the most vulnerable communities, further widening existing inequalities and leading to increased poverty, famine, and displacement. In nations where farming is the primary means of providing for oneself, such as developing countries, the effects of climate change, such as droughts and floods, may result in crop damage, food scarcity, and an increase in malnourishment (FAO, 2020). Moreover, severe weather situations such as hurricanes, wildfires, and floods have catastrophic effects on societies, resulting in fatalities, relocation, and financial harm as expressed by the IPCC in 2018.

Climate change is a universal concern that impacts nations in varying ways. Certain countries face a greater susceptibility to the consequences of emissions, whereas certain countries have a greater responsibility for emitting greenhouse gases. It is crucial for all nations to take swift and assertive measures to address this problem and avert its most severe outcomes.

Small island developing countries (SIDS) are at a high risk of experiencing the consequences of climate change, such as the rise in sea-levels, ocean acidification, and severe weather conditions (UNDESA, 2021). Tuvalu, a nation located in the Pacific Island, is facing a serious threat of flooding and contamination of its freshwater resources due to the constant increase in sea levels, as reported by the UNDP in 2021. The Caribbean has been experiencing a rise in both the number and intensity of hurricanes, leading to major infrastructure damage and disrupting the crucial tourism industry, which serves as a key source of income for several nations in the area (UNEP, 2021). These countries require urgent and robust measures to adjust to the effects of climate change and diminish their susceptibilities.

However, certain countries carry a larger obligation to decrease their levels of greenhouse gas emissions. According to the World Resources Institute's report in 2021, the three leading contributors of greenhouse gas emissions worldwide are the United States, China, and the European Union. These nations have a pressing need to swiftly and courageously adopt measures that will curtail their carbon footprint and shift towards environmentally-friendly economies. The European Union has established environmental goals to decrease emissions by a minimum of 55% by the year 2030 and attain a state of net-zero emissions by 2050, according to the European Commission's (2020) plan. China has vowed to reach the pinnacle of its emissions by 2030 and accomplish carbon neutrality by 2060, according to Xinhua (2020). The White House, in 2021, has committed to reducing the United States' emissions by 50-52% by 2030 by rejoining the Paris Agreement.

Moreover, a plethora of developing nations are encountering considerable hurdles in harmonizing their economic progression with their obligation to curtail carbon emissions. India continues to heavily depend on coal as its primary source of energy despite being the third-largest contributor of greenhouse gas emissions globally, as per the IEA 2021 report. India has established ambitious objectives to enhance its renewable energy potential and decrease the intensity of its outflows (Government of India, 2021). Numerous African countries are struggling to provide modern energy services while also reducing their emissions, according to IRENA's report from 2020. Smart and effective measures are needed by these countries to shift towards sustainable and low-carbon economies while making sure that their developmental requirements are fulfilled.

Immediate and courageous measures are necessary on all fronts, encompassing individuals, governmental bodies, and enterprises. According to the IPCC (2018), the strategy involves several measures such as utilizing sustainable energy resources, enhancing energy efficacy, and funding low-emissions infrastructure as a way of mitigating carbon emissions. This also entails altering the way we consume resources and minimizing unnecessary waste, while simultaneously supporting climate adaptation strategies that aid vulnerable communities in coping with the effects of climate change (IPCC, 2018). The implementation of policies that endorse sustainable living and encourage businesses to adopt low-carbon technologies can be greatly facilitated by the government, as stated by the IPCC in 2018.

Swift and decisive measures are imperative to tackle climate change and avert its disastrous consequences on our planet and all living beings. Every country needs to consider their own individual conditions and issues, and create strategies to lower their greenhouse gas emissions, adjust to the consequences of climate change, and switch to eco-friendly and low-emission economies. If we don't take action soon, the consequences for the planet and future generations will be extremely severe.

The Necessity of a Just Transition to a Low-Carbon Economy

The urgent need to shift towards a low-carbon economy has intensified as a result of the catastrophic effects of climate change. It is essential to ensure a just and impartial shift so that marginalized groups and employees do not get marginalized. A just conversion involves an intentional and fair course of action that ensures that employees, societies, and sectors that will be significantly impacted by the shift towards a sustainable economy are not neglected. Addressing the social and economic outcomes of this shift including unemployment, job cuts, and the displacement of susceptible groups is indispensable.

The idea of a fair transition is becoming increasingly popular around the world, and numerous countries have begun to integrate it into their strategies for tackling climate change. The European Union has promised that a just transition will be a significant element of its European Green Deal, with the provision of a €100 billion Fair Move Component aimed at supporting the people and industries in regions that are most impacted by the transition. According to the European Commission's latest report, 2021. The National Fair Transition Methodology in South Africa is designed to guarantee that the coal industry's communities and employees go through a just and equitable phase of transition. Likewise, Canada has instituted a Task Force on Equitable Transition to provide proposals for a just shift towards a low-carbon economic system. (The Canadian government of 2018).

In addition, there exist many groups and undertakings that promote a just and equitable shift. The ITUC has initiated an effort to ensure that climate action prioritizes workers and communities with its Just Transition campaign. The Climate Justice Alliance, comprised of several American organizations, aims to establish a balanced shift towards an environmentally friendly and fair economy that benefits everyone. Efforts have been made to ensure a sustainable future for all by adopting a holistic approach and prioritizing social justice in the transition to a low-carbon economy.

Numerous nations have enforced strategies intended to achieve an equitable shift towards an economy that emits a lesser amount of carbon. Argentina's legislation on Climate Change includes provisions that prioritize a just shift to a low-carbon economy, taking into account the socio-economic implications of the transition. The legislation establishes a country-wide initiative to foster the growth of renewable energy with the objectives of generating fresh employment opportunities, stimulating sustainable economic advancement, and easing the transition for staff and localities dependent on fossil fuels. In 2018, the Ministry of Environment and Sustainable Development in Argentina was responsible for the management and promotion of sustainable practices.

Australia's governing body has created the National Framework for Energy Efficiency, which comprises actions to tackle the societal and financial effects of shifting towards a less-polluting economy. The structure entails a range of measures, comprising of training and job opportunities for employees in the sector of renewable energy as well as assistance for communities impacted by these changes. (Australian Government, 2015) made this statement.

In addition, the importance of a fair transition has been acknowledged by the UNFCCC under the Paris Agreement. The accord acknowledges the necessity of enhancing nations' capacity to adapt to the consequences of global warming, such as by carrying out an equitable switch to an eco-friendly economy. The convention of the United Nations Framework regarding climate change in 2015.

As a whole, the notion of an equitable shift is becoming increasingly popular around the world as numerous nations and groups come to appreciate the need to confront the societal and financial impact of moving towards an economy with minimal carbon emissions. The aforementioned instances illustrate the feasibility of a fair transition which can be realized by synergizing policy actions, constructive communication, and cooperative effort among authorities, laborers, localities, and other involved parties.

Despite progress made, significant efforts are needed to ensure that the shift towards a low-carbon economy is fair and impartial. Sustaining economic growth in the renewable energy sector necessitates persistent endeavors to cater to the requirements and apprehensions of marginalized communities and laborers. It also requires devising policies and schemes that encourage sustainable job creation. By collaborating, we can bring about an equitable shift towards an economy with reduced carbon emissions, which would lead to a sustainable future for generations to follow.

The Potential Benefits of Addressing Climate Change

Taking action to address environmental change has the potential to bring numerous benefits to both humanity and the natural environment. One of the major benefits is the mitigation of the impacts of climate change, such as rising sea levels, more frequent and severe natural disasters, and alteration to precipitation trends. The IPCC recommends decreasing the release of greenhouse gases as a means of decreasing the likelihood and impact of negative consequences associated with climate change.

Taking action on climate change can also result in enhancements in the well-being of the general public. For instance, the promotion of clean air and the mitigation of respiratory illnesses can be tackled by means of decreasing air contamination and transitioning to sustainable energy alternatives. In essence, air quality can be enhanced and various advantages such as preserving biodiversity, minimizing soil erosion, and managing water currents can be achieved by decreasing deforestation and encouraging reforestation, according to the EPA (2021).

Moreover, taking measures to address climate change can bring about beneficial effects on the economy. As an example, the transition towards a low-carbon economy may lead to the emergence of fresh employment opportunities related to renewable energy and energy conservation. Enhanced economic progress can be achieved particularly in underdeveloped countries by making substantial investments in renewable energy sources, as per the United Nations Environment Programme's (UNEP) report in 2021.

Vulnerable groups including low-income communities, indigenous populations and developing nations are disproportionately affected by the effects of climate change. In order to tackle the issue of climate change, it is vital to diminish these disparities and foster a fair and impartial community (IPCC, 2018).

Enhancing energy security can be seen as a positive consequence of taking action on climate change. By enhancing their energy independence, nations can decrease their reliance on fossil fuels and minimize vulnerability to fluctuations in the worldwide energy market. The potential advantages of this could be immense for countries that greatly depend on oil and gas imports, particularly in terms of economic and national security aspects (as per IEA, 2020).

Taking action on climate change could result in betterment of food security as well. The food systems across the world might undergo substantial consequences due to climate change, including modifications in crop harvests, variations in the distribution of aquatic life, and changes in the occurrence and intensity of natural calamities. Governments can enhance their ability to withstand the consequences of climate change and safeguard the sustenance of their people by supporting eco-friendly agricultural techniques and allocating resources towards exploring new innovations (FAO, 2016).

Tackling climate change can foster advancement and development of technology and imaginative ideas. Innovation in renewable energy, energy storage, and related technologies is crucial for achieving a shift towards a low-carbon economy. Countries can establish fresh markets, create novel economic possibilities, and take the lead in technological advancements by investing in these technologies, as per the WRI 2021 report.

Undoubtedly, taking action to combat climate change can result in significant advantages for both culture and society. We can advance a culture that is both sustainable and fair by encouraging sustainable behaviors and lifestyles, resulting in a decreased environmental impact on human society. The result of this can be progress in well-being, health, and quality of life, as well as advances in general social and cultural growth (UNESCO, 2021).

Chapter 9

Solutions to Global Warming

Our planet is heavily influenced by the way we choose to live our lives. Our actions are significant. Approximately two-thirds of overall greenhouse gas emissions globally stem from private households. There are multiple factors that influence an individual's "carbon footprint," which refers to the amount of greenhouse gas emissions linked to their daily activities. These factors may include the food they consume, the means of transportation they use, the products they buy, and the electricity they consume.

By the year 2030, there should be a 50% reduction in the release of ozone-depleting substances, and by the year 2050, there should be no such substance released for the maintenance of a sustainable environment. Swift and extensive measures of great importance are imperative for both governments and businesses to take. The transition towards a low-carbon world undoubtedly necessitates the cooperation of the general public, particularly in developed countries.

Although it may seem like a daunting task, there are ways to tackle this issue and mitigate the pace at which the planet is heating up. In this chapter we will delve into various approaches that can be employed to address the issue of global warming, such as advocating for energy conservation, financing advancements in sustainable energy sources, endorsing policies that lessen carbon discharges, and some additional means. By implementing these strategies globally, the planet's increasing temperatures can potentially be remedied.

The Importance of Decreasing Greenhouse Gas Emissions

The ongoing difficulty that mankind is grappling with is the issue of worldwide climate change, which is having detrimental impacts on both the welfare of individuals and the natural habitat as a consequence of rising temperatures. The primary cause of global warming is the accumulation of greenhouse gases, particularly carbon dioxide, which is emitted during the burning of fossil fuels. Alternative gases such as methane, nitrous oxide, and fluorinated gases also play a significant role in intensifying the greenhouse effect. The gases present in the atmosphere for a prolonged period may have a long-lasting impact on increasing temperatures for a considerable amount of time, ranging from several decades to centuries.

Reducing the emission of greenhouse gases is crucial to slowing down the progression of global warming. In order to avert disastrous consequences resulting from climate change, the IPCC has recommended the necessity of restricting global warming to a mere 1 degree. It is crucial to achieve the objective of reducing greenhouse gas emissions by a significant degree, with urgency and immediacy, in order to reach a temperature of 5°C.

Climate change is a widespread phenomenon with significant effects across various parts of the world, leading to the melting of glaciers and rising sea levels that affect numerous regions and populations. The negative effects of extreme weather conditions such as heatwaves, droughts, and floods are becoming more frequent and severe, causing significant consequences for economies and societies. Moreover, the rise in temperatures across the world could have adverse effects on agriculture, food security, water sources, and biodiversity, culminating in catastrophic events on a global scale. To mitigate the effects of global warming, it is crucial to swiftly decrease the emission of detrimental greenhouse gases.

Limiting the utilization of fossil fuels, which are the primary sources of carbon dioxide emissions, is an essential step in reducing greenhouse gas emissions. According to the EIA (2021), there could be a significant reduction in emissions by replacing non-renewable sources like fossil fuels with renewable energy options like wind and solar power. The 2021 report from UNEP suggests that implementing intelligent energy management strategies like improving safety measures and adopting more efficient equipment can lead to a reduction in energy consumption and emissions. Advocating for eco-friendly modes of transportation like electric vehicles, biking, and taking public transit can significantly decrease emissions.

Reducing greenhouse gas emissions can bring about numerous advantages. According to WHO (2018), reducing the consumption of fossil fuels has the potential to improve air quality and alleviate asthma and other respiratory ailments. By embracing sustainable energy sources, we can create fresh employment openings and diminish our reliance on imported fossil fuels, ultimately strengthening our energy security. This assertion was made by IRENA in 2021. In addition, sustainable economic growth can be achieved by directing resources towards renewable energy and simultaneously curbing harmful pollutants. In 2021, the UNDP declared that this results in a win-win situation for both the economy and the environment.

Increasing Renewable Energy Sources

Energy is at the core of the environmental challenge and key to the arrangement. A considerable portion of the ozone-depleting substances that sweep the Earth and trap the sun's intensity is created through energy creation by consuming petroleum products to produce power and intensity.

Fossil fuels like coal, oil, and gas, which account for over 75% of global emissions of greenhouse gases and nearly 90% of all emissions of carbon dioxide, are the most important aspect of worldwide environmental change.

The research is conclusive: to stay away from the most obviously terrible effects of environmental change, discharges should be decreased by close to half by 2030 and arrive at net zero by 2050.

We must end our reliance on fossil fuels and invest in clean, accessible, affordable, long-lasting, and dependable alternative energy sources to accomplish this.

Petroleum derivatives actually represent in excess of 80% of worldwide energy creation, however cleaner wellsprings of energy are making strides. Currently, renewable energy accounts for approximately 29% of all electricity.

Renewable energy sources are pivotal in reducing greenhouse gas emissions and mitigating the impacts of global warming. The use of renewable energy has been on the rise globally, driven by factors such as declining costs, government incentives, and environmental awareness.

In order to increase the use of renewable energy sources, policy support from the government is essential. To establish targets and regulations for renewable energy, governments can offer projects utilizing renewable energy incentives like tax credits, grants, and subsidies. The Investment Tax Credit (ITC) and the Production Tax Credit (PTC) are two examples of incentives provided by the US government to encourage the growth of wind and solar power (SEIA, 2021). In the same way, China has set an objective of accomplishing 35% of its all-out energy utilization from non-fossil sources by 2030 (REN21, 2020).

Besides, technological advancements are crucial for expanding the utilization of renewable energy sources. Renewable energy may become more competitive with fossil fuels as a result of the development of technologies that are both more effective and less expensive, such as wind turbines and solar panels. Moreover, the intermittent nature of renewable energy sources can be overcome by innovations in energy storage technologies like hydrogen storage and batteries. For instance, Tesla's Powerwall battery framework empowers mortgage holders to store an abundance of sun-based energy during the day and use it around evening time (Tesla).

Many corporations are setting sustainable goals that include the use of renewable energy sources. Corporations can invest in their renewable energy projects or purchase renewable energy from third-party providers, helping to advance the demand for renewable energy sources. For instance, Google has committed to sourcing 100% of its energy from renewable sources by 2030 (Google, 2021). Similarly, Ikea has installed over 1 million solar panels in its stores and warehouses globally (Ikea).

Grid integration is another important factor in increasing the use of renewable energy sources. Due to the intermittent nature of renewable energy sources, there may be issues with grid stability and reliability as more renewable energy sources are added to the grid. Grid operators are increasingly turning to smart grid technologies, which can assist in managing and balancing energy supply and demand, as a means of overcoming this obstacle. Energy storage systems, on the other hand, have the ability to provide additional capacity during peak times, and demand response programs, for instance, can encourage customers to reduce their electricity consumption during times of high demand (IEA, 2020).

Community solar programs can also help increase the use of renewable energy sources. These programs allow multiple customers to share the benefits of a single solar project, such as reduced energy costs or access to clean energy, without the need for individual rooftop solar installations. Community solar programs can help increase the accessibility of renewable energy to a wider range of customers, including renters and low-income households (SEIA, 2021).

Offshore wind is a promising area for expanding the utilize of renewable energy sources. Offshore wind turbines can capture stronger and more consistent winds, providing a more solid source of renewable energy. Also, offshore wind turbines can be placed further from shore, reducing visual and noise impacts on nearby communities. However, offshore wind projects can be more expensive and technically challenging to construct than onshore wind projects. Nevertheless, offshore wind is anticipated to play a significant role in expanding the utilization of renewable energy sources in the coming years (IRENA, 2020).

Taking Energy Efficiency Measures

In theory, the path to energy efficiency is a sustainability race. When a system is more efficient, less fuel is needed to produce a given amount of energy, resulting in lower costs for the service provider and lower prices for customers. - Jens Martin Skibsted

Energy effectiveness is characterized as utilizing less energy to provide a similar item or service, like lighting, heating, and transportation. One of the two pillars of sustainable energy policy is the shift to renewable energy sources and the improvement of energy efficiency.

Energy efficiency is essential for ensuring a safe and reliable reduction in energy consumption and emissions of greenhouse gases because it is a cheap and abundant resource that is found in all nations, rich and poor. Additionally, the quickest and cheapest solution to the climate crisis is unquestionably improvement in energy efficiency.

Industry, transportation, homes and buildings, recycling, and other areas where the greatest energy savings can be made have been identified by experts in energy efficiency around the world.

The International Energy Agency (IEA) has expressed that superior energy proficiency in modern cycles, transportation, and buildings could prompt a 30% decrease in the planet's energy needs by 2050 and assist with controlling global discharges of greenhouse gases.

Any strategy to reduce greenhouse gas emissions and lessen the effects of climate change must include energy efficiency (U.S. Environmental Protection Agency).

Home modifications are one-way individuals can implement energy efficiency measures. For instance, reducing the amount of energy required to heat, cool, and power a home can be accomplished by installing energy-efficient appliances, upgrading windows and doors, and improving insulation. Smart home technology and programmable thermostats can also assist homeowners in better monitoring and controlling their energy consumption (U.S. Department of Energy, 2022).

Energy efficiency measures can also be beneficial to businesses. A company's bottom line can be improved and energy costs reduced by, upgrading lighting and HVAC systems, implementing energy management systems, and increasing manufacturing process efficiency. Besides, many businesses are turning to renewable energy sources like wind and solar power to meet their energy needs. (International Energy Agency, 2021).

In industrial settings, energy efficiency measures are also important. For instance, reducing energy consumption in manufacturing processes can be aided by increasing the efficiency of motors, pumps, and other equipment. Moreover, streamlining production network coordination factors and diminishing waste can assist in decreasing how much energy is expected to be used to deliver and ship merchandise (U.S. Department of Energy, 2021).

Energy efficiency measures can also provide a variety of other benefits, in addition to the advantages of lowering energy consumption and reducing the effects of climate change. Reduced energy consumption can help improve air quality by lowering emissions from energy production. The measures to improve energy efficiency may contribute to the creation of employment opportunities in energy management, building retrofitting, and renewable energy sectors (U.S. Department of Energy, 2021).

Apart from that, energy proficiency measures can likewise improve the solace and reasonableness of homes and working environments. For instance, a more comfortable indoor environment can be made possible by upgrading heating and cooling systems and improving insulation. Likewise, redesigning lighting and executing daylighting systems can assist with making a more charming and useful work area (U.S. Department of Energy, 2022).

Energy efficiency measures have many advantages, but there are also some drawbacks to consider. For example, the upfront expenses of updating hardware or executing new systems can be a boundary for certain people and associations. Moreover, there might be an absence of data or skills accessible to help execute energy effectiveness measures. Notwithstanding, there are numerous assets accessible, including government impetuses, supporting choices, and energy reviews, that can assist people and associations with defeating these difficulties. (U.S. Department of Energy, 2022)

There is still a lot of work to be done in the area of energy efficiency and lowering emissions of greenhouse gases, despite the impressive progress that has been made in recent years, and we cannot afford to be complacent. Al Gore said, "If we don't act now, future generations will look at us and say, "You knew this—you knew what was going to happen to the planet, and you decided to ignore it?"

Carbon Capture and Storage

The process of storing carbon dioxide (CO2) emissions from power plants, industrial facilities, and other sources underground or in other long-term storage options is known as carbon capture and storage (CCS). CCS has the potential to significantly reduce emissions of greenhouse gases and mitigate the effects of climate change. (U.S. Department of Energy, 2021)

There are several steps in the CCS process. CO2 is first extracted from the source, which might be an industrial facility or power plant. The captured CO2 is then moved to a storage location, usually by pipeline or another means of transportation. Finally, the carbon dioxide is stored in deep geological formations like depleted oil and gas reservoirs or in long-term storage options like saline aquifers. (E.P.A. of the United States)

CCS has the potential to be used in many different settings. CCS technology can be used to capture and store CO2 emissions from power plants, which are a significant source. Moreover, CCS can be utilized to capture and store emissions from industrial processes like cement production and steel manufacturing. CCS can likewise be enforced in the oil and gas industry, where CO2 can be infused into oil fields to upgrade oil recuperation while additionally putting the CO2 underground. (U.S. Branch of Energy, 2021)

While CCS can possibly play a basic role in diminishing ozone-harming substance outflows, there are also difficulties related to executing the innovation. Implementing CCS, for instance, can be costly, particularly when retrofitting existing facilities. Additionally, there are concerns regarding the long-term storage of CO2, including the requirement for ongoing monitoring and upkeep of storage sites and the possibility of leaks. (E.P.A. of the United States)

There are numerous ongoing efforts to develop and implement CCS technology in spite of these obstacles. These efforts include demonstration projects to test the technology in real-world settings and research and development to increase CCS' efficiency and cost-effectiveness. CCS technology development and deployment can also be aided by government policies and incentives. (U.S. Division of Energy, 2021)

A few nations all over the world are seeking carbon capture and storage (CCS) innovations as a method for reducing greenhouse gas emissions and addressing climate change.

One model is Norway, which has invested vigorously in CCS innovation and is home to the world's most memorable full-scale CCS office, the Sleipner Venture. CO2 from the production of natural gas is stored in a saline aquifer deep beneath the North Sea by the Sleipner Project. Since its introduction in 1996, the technology has successfully reduced natural gas production process emissions (IEA, 2021).

Another model is Canada, which has executed a few enormous-scope CCS projects, remembering the Mission CCS office for Alberta. The CO2 that comes from a large oil sand upgrading facility is taken in by the Quest project and stored deep underground. Since its inception in 2015, the project has been able to capture and store more than one million metric tons of CO2 annually (Natural Resources Canada, 2021).

In the US, there are a few huge-scope CCS projects in activity or improvement, remembering the Petra Nova CCS office for Texas. Petra Nova stores CO2 in a deep saline aquifer after capturing it from a coal-fired power plant. The undertaking has been in activity since around 2017 and has the ability to catch and stockpile 1.6 million tons of CO2 each year (U.S. Branch of Energy, 2021).

China is additionally putting resources into CCS innovation, with a few huge-scope projects in activity or improvement. For instance, the GreenGen project in Tianjin captures CO2 from a coal gasification plant and uses it to create power. Up to 600,000 tons of CO2 can be captured and stored annually by the project, which has been in operation since 2018 (IEA, 2021).

Overall, CCS is an innovation with the possibility of playing a basic role in reducing greenhouse gas substance discharges and moderating the effects of climate change. The oil and gas industry, power plants, industrial facilities, and a variety of other settings are all potential applications for the technology. Even though putting CCS into use can be difficult, ongoing efforts to improve the technology and the support of the government can help overcome these obstacles and encourage the use of CCS as part of a comprehensive strategy to combat climate change.

Policy Interventions to Reduce Emissions

Policy interventions play a pivotal role in lessening greenhouse gas emissions and relieving climate change. To address this problem, a variety of policies, including targets for renewable energy and emissions trading schemes, have been implemented by governments globally.

One example of policy intervention is the European Union's Emissions Trading System (ETS). The ETS is a cap-and-trade system that restricts certain industries' ability to emit CO2 emissions. Companies that produce more carbon dioxide than their disbursed quantity are required to collect emissions allowances from agencies that produce much less carbon dioxide. Companies are encouraged to invest in low-carbon technologies and reduce their emissions as a result of this financial incentive (European Commission, 2021).

The Renewable Energy Target (RET) set by the United Kingdom is another example. The Renewable Energy Target (RET) policy mandates that a predetermined proportion of electricity be generated from renewable sources. The goal was set at 5.5 percent in 2005 and has since been raised to 30 percent by 2020. The UK's renewable energy production has grown as a result of the policy (UK Government, 2021).

In the transportation area, many countries have executed strategies to boost the reception of electric vehicles (EVs). For instance, Norway has a number of policies in place to encourage the use of electric vehicles, such as the exclusion of the vehicle registration tax, reductions in tolls, and access to bus lanes. Over half of all new car sales in Norway in 2020 were electric vehicles as a result of these policies (Norwegian Ministry of Climate and Environment, 2021).

Carbon pricing, incentives for renewable energy, and regulations that limit emissions from industrial sources are some of the most effective policy interventions. However, there are a wide range of other possible interventions.

Either through a tax or a cap-and-trade system, carbon pricing is an economic tool for pricing carbon emissions. This provides monetary motivation for organizations and individuals to decrease their carbon footprint and put resources into cleaner innovations. Nations that have carried out carbon estimating include Sweden, Switzerland, and Canada, which has a public carbon valuing framework that applies a carbon duty or discharges an exchanging framework to regions that don't have their own carbon valuing framework (Government of Canada, 2021).

Incentives for renewable energy help finance the creation and implementation of clean energy technologies like wind and solar power. Feed-in tariffs, which guarantee a fixed price for electricity generated by renewable sources, have been implemented in Germany and Spain. This has contributed to the expansion of renewable energy in these nations and provides producers of renewable energy with a steady source of revenue (International Energy Agency, 2021).

Modern guidelines can also be effective in decreasing emissions from enormous modern sources, for example, power plants and production lines. The Environmental Protection Agency (EPA) in the United States has enacted a number of regulations to restrict power plants' and other industrial sources' emissions of greenhouse gases and other pollutants. The Clean Air Act, which regulates emissions from industrial sources and sets national ambient air quality standards, and the Clean Power Plan, which limits power plant carbon emissions, are examples of these regulations (EPA, 2021).

Policy interventions have the potential to reduce emissions of greenhouse gases, but they can also face difficulties and limitations. Political opposition, financial obstacles, and technological constraints are among the obstacles and limitations of emissions reduction policy interventions. Differences in political ideology or the influence of vested interests can lead to political opposition. The potential economic effects on industries and consumers, as well as the cost of implementing and enforcing policies, are examples of economic barriers. Mechanical requirements might incorporate the accessibility and cost of clean energy innovations, as well as the requirement for a new framework to help their arrangement.

Effective communication and education are essential for gaining political support for policy interventions in order to overcome these obstacles and limitations. Building coalitions and engaging stakeholders can also aid in gaining support for policies. In order to overcome obstacles related to the economy, clean energy technology development and deployment may necessitate the application of financial subsidies and incentives. It might likewise be important to investigate new financing instruments, like green bonds, to help the transition to a low-carbon economy. Finally, in order to overcome technological limitations, it may be necessary to make an investment in research and development in order to enhance the affordability and effectiveness of clean energy technologies.

Despite these difficulties and limitations, the effective examples presented above demonstrate that policy interventions can reduce greenhouse gas emissions in a variety of settings. However, a variety of factors, such as political will, economic conditions, and technological advancements, can influence these policies' efficacy. Policy interventions can be studied and evaluated on a regular basis to ensure that they are successful in reducing emissions and preventing climate change.

Chapter 10

Hindrance to Global Warming Solutions

According to Christopher Knittel of MIT Sloan, climate change is a global problem whose resolution necessitates a phenomenal position of mindfulness and immolation.

Changes in climate the maturity of the world concurs that it's a threat, yet how would we overpower it? What is keeping us down? In a recent interview, Christopher Knittel, an applied economics professor at the MIT Sloan School of Management, linked five of the top obstacles.

"The first crucial point of climate change that puts it at odds with former environmental issues is that it's a global contaminant, rather than a original contaminant. " (Climate change)" It does the same damage to the world whether I release a ton of CO2 in London or Cambridge, Massachusetts," Knittel stated. Balance that with neighborhood venoms, where on the off chance that I discharge a lot of sulfur dioxide or nitrogen oxide in Cambridge, most of the detriment stays close to Cambridge."

As a result, controlling CO2 is significantly more grueling.

The majority of contaminants that contribute to climate change will be detrimental in the future, so climate change remains academic for the time being. This indicates that our maturity won't actually be affected by climate change; rather, it's an academic script presented in maps and graphs. We hope that altruism inspires politicians and choosers, but this isn't always the case. In general, there's little pressure on policymakers to act.

People who stand to suffer the most from climate change aren't yet born. According to Knittel," going back to the policymaker's perspective, she has much lower incitement to reduce hothouse gas emigrations because those reductions are going to profit choosers in the future and not her current choosers," which means that she has a much lower incitement to do so.

According to Knittel, despite the global trouble posed by adulterants that alter climate, scientists find it delicate to link them to a specific environmental disaster. Disbelievers find it easier to ignore or deny the effects of climate change when there's no clear cause.

Non-industrial nations add to a huge portion of impurity
Principally, this is not their main concern.

"We're asking veritably poor nations, who are concerned about whether they will be suitable to shoot their children to academy or where their coming mess will come from, to pay for the reduction of hothouse gas emigrations for the benefit of the world. And that's a delicate task for a policymaker in a developing nation," he stated.

It's hard to accept that ultramodern conveniences like air conditioning, electricity, and transportation each contribute to climate change and that the results may bear significant offerings and a shift in life.

"Despite the fact that we have seen extraordinary reductions in solar-powered charges and batteries for electric vehicles, these are as yet expensive alternatives. When it comes to confronting climate change, there's no free lunch," Knittel advised.

Knittel wrote lately in the Los Angeles Times," Those five factors would have made climate change a brilliant choice if an evil genius had set out to design the perfect environmental extremity." In any case, we did not bear a despicable virtuoso. We discovered it by accident. (MIT Management Slogan School, 2019)

Effective solutions to mitigate the effects of global warming encounter a number of obstacles, despite the growing recognition of the urgency of the issue. These range from political and economic boundaries to technological constraints and social opposition. In this chapter, we'll look at some of the biggest problems and limitations of emissions-reduction policy interventions and possible ways to get around them. By comprehending and addressing these obstacles, we can work toward a more sustainable future and preserve our planet for future generations.

Political Barriers to Action

Political boundaries to activity on climate change have been a critical obstacle to carrying out compelling techniques and measures to reduce greenhouse gas releases. The issue of political will is one of the biggest deterrents. It is frequently impacted by short-term political interests, the impact of fossil fuel industries, and ideological differences among policymakers.

For instance, many politicians center on temporal economic advancement over long-haul natural sustainability and may contradict making a move on environmental change because of worries about its expected financial impact (Dolsak and Prakash, 2018). Furthermore, political polarization can result in a climate policy impasse because politicians may be more concerned with defeating their adversaries than with coming to an agreement with both parties. This can bring about a lack of agreement on the requirement for and reasonable procedure for environmental change.

Moreover, in a few countries, the polarization of climate change as a partisan issue has hampered climate change action. Some politicians and intrigued groups have denied climate change's existence or the need for action, subsequently politicizing the issue. According to (McCright & Dunlap, The Politicization of Climate Change and Polarization in the American Public's Views of Global Warming, 2001–2010, 2011), this has resulted in a need for agreement and expanded political polarization, making it challenging to execute significant climate action. Political polarization exists in a number of countries, including Brazil, Australia, and the United States, so this problem affects more than just one nation or region.

Intrigued groups and campaign finance may also have an impact on political barriers in some instances (Skocpol & Williamson, 2012). For instance, fossil fuel organizations might campaign against environmental techniques that may undermine their benefits, while individuals and associations that focus on environmental activity might not have a similar degree of financial resources to make their voices heard. The implementation of effective climate policies may be further complicated by these factors.

Moreover, due to its political nature, climate change is frequently the subject of partisan political debate, with political ideologies significantly influencing attitudes toward climate action. For instance, conservative politicians in many countries have been less willing to support policies to address climate change and have been more skeptical of climate science.

The unwillingness of politicians to make decisions that are not popular is one of the biggest political barriers to taking action on climate change. In many cases, the actions anticipated to reduce greenhouse gas emissions are politically repulsive, as they frequently include forcing costs on businesses and people. A carbon tax, for instance, can be politically challenging to implement because businesses and individuals who will bear the tax's costs are likely to restrict it. Policies that are required to address climate change may be difficult to execute due to this reluctance to make decisions that are not popular (Gupta et al., 2010).

One of the political obstructions to taking action on environmental change is the absence of political will. This can be caused by a number of things, such as the short-term focus of electoral cycles, competing political priorities, and the perceived cost of taking action. Lawmakers could be reluctant to make a move on environmental change assuming that they see that the costs of action are excessively high and that there are distinctive issues that are seriously pressing in the minds of voters. This absence of political will can make it difficult to carry out the arrangements that are important to address environmental change.

Another obstacle to action is the difficulty of reaching international agreements on climate policy due to divergent national interests and priorities. This was demonstrated by the failure of the 2009 United Nations Climate Change Conference in Copenhagen to reach a legally binding international agreement on reducing emissions. Although the ensuing Paris Agreement, which was reached in 2015, represents a significant progression in global climate governance, many experts contend that it is inadequate to prevent catastrophic climate change.

Moreover, issues of social justice and equity can also be a political hindrance to natural action. There is a frequent conflict between developed and developing countries regarding the allocation of responsibility for reducing emissions and providing financing for adaptation because climate change disproportionately affects marginalized communities and developing nations (Schlosberg & Collins, 2014). A commitment to inclusive and participatory decision-making processes that involve marginalized communities and a recognition of the historical and structural inequalities that have contributed to the unequal distribution of climate impacts and resources are necessary for addressing these issues.

Regardless, there have also been instances of political initiative and activity on environmental change. The European Union has been a pioneer in climate policy, investing in renewable energy and building up ambitious objectives for bringing down greenhouse gas emissions (European Commission, 2021). Despite being the largest emitter of greenhouse gases, China has implemented policies to reduce emissions and invested intensely in renewable energy to combat climate change. In the US, a few states have carried out their own environmental procedures, and there have been endeavors to advance environmental action at the local level.

Despite these political hindrances to taking action on environmental change, there are examples of nations that have taken noteworthy steps to resolve the issue. Germany, which has emerged as a market leader in renewable energy, is one such illustration. A number of policies have been implemented in Germany, one of which has been a feed-in tariff program that has empowered the growth of renewable energy sources. Subsequently, sustainable power presently represents more than 30% of the power age in Germany (BMWi, 2021).

Costa Rica, for example, has set a goal of becoming carbon neutral by 2050. Renewable energy now accounts for over 98% of Costa Rica's power generation, indicating that the country has already made significant progress toward this objective (UNDP, 2021). Costa Rica has carried out a range of strategies, including a carbon charge and a prohibition on new oil investigations, to accomplish its carbon neutrality goal.

To beat these political hindrances to environmental action, it is important to engage with diverse stakeholders, including civil society groups, businesses, and governments, and to foster creative organization procedures that go beyond traditional top-down methodologies (Bulkeley et al., 2014). This may require the creation of novel models of global governance that are more democratic, inclusive, and responsive to the requirements of all stakeholders (Steffen et al., 2015). Moreover, it requires a willingness to challenge and transform existing power structures that maintain the status quo as well as a recognition of the need for systemic change. Eventually, addressing the political boundaries of environmental action requires a blend of crucial action, political will, and public support to create an additional equitable and sustainable future.

Economic Barriers to Action

It is widely acknowledged that climate change poses a significant threat to humanity. Although there are numerous solutions to combating what the United Nations has dubbed the "existential threat" of our time, it is still not entirely clear how these solutions will be paid for.

While investments in sustainable infrastructure and renewable energy are on the rise, more money will be spent on fossil fuels from January 2020 to March 2021 because, when they are burned, they produce the harmful gases that are driving climate change.

A lot of countries don't have the money to switch to clean energy and a sustainable way of life that could stop climate change. The United Nations claims that climate finance is the solution because there are significant opportunities for investors and because not investing will cost even more in the long run.

Economic barriers to climate action vary across nations and regions. Due to their already-hot climates and lack of resources for adaptation efforts, developing countries in Africa, South Asia, and Latin America are particularly vulnerable to the effects of climate change. Many of these nations also lack the financial resources to transition to clean energy and a sustainable way of life that could reverse climate change. The United Nations has called for significant investments in climate finance and international cooperation to address this gap. (UN News, Global Perspective Human Stories)

The high cost of moving to a low-carbon economy is one of the biggest economic obstacles to taking action on climate change. Wind and solar power infrastructure development requires significant upfront investment costs. On the other hand, conventional energy sources like oil and coal are less expensive in the short term. Thus, many countries and organizations might be reluctant to put resources into renewable energy because of the apparent significant expense (Peters and Hertwich, 2008).

One more economic hindrance to activity on climate change is the issue of seriousness. Nations that carry out severe climate policies might be in a difficult spot compared to those that don't. For example, countries that have to pay more to cut emissions may have to pay more for energy, which will make their goods more expensive and less competitive in global markets. This issue can prompt a "rush to the base," where nations are hesitant to execute environmental policies inspired by a paranoid fear of losing their upper hand.

Besides, businesses do not receive sufficient financial incentives to reduce their emissions. Businesses may be enticed financially to reduce their emissions through carbon pricing mechanisms like carbon taxes or emissions trading schemes. However, many nations lack these mechanisms, and those that do may not have set the carbon price sufficiently high to encourage businesses to reduce emissions. Businesses may choose short-term profits over long-term sustainability as a result of this.

The absence of incentives for businesses to reduce their carbon emissions is another economic barrier to global warming action. This is in addition to market failures. Companies may lack the financial incentive to invest in cleaner technologies or modify their production procedures to reduce emissions if there is no carbon price. This is especially true in sectors like energy and transportation, where fossil fuels are deeply ingrained. For instance, the oil and gas industry have a strong political impact, and numerous states have hesitated to execute policies that would adversely influence these businesses, such as a carbon tax.

Additionally, putting policies in place to combat climate change can be costly, which can make it difficult to take action. In many cases, the upfront expenses of carrying out clean energy or energy effectiveness measures might be high, and the advantages may not be promptly apparent. This can be really difficult for non-industrial nations, where the expenses of progressing to low-carbon economies might be prohibitively expensive (Dechezleprêtre et al., 2010).

However, there are examples of nations that, despite these economic obstacles, have successfully implemented policies to combat climate change while also generating economic benefits. For example, Germany's Energiewende, or energy transition, has made positions and stimulated economic growth by putting resources into environmentally friendly power innovations and energy effectiveness measures. Similarly, Costa Rica has carried out an effective program to progress to sustainable power, which has made positions and diminished the country's reliance on imported fossil fuel derivatives. Through innovative policies and investments that generate economic benefits, these examples demonstrate that overcoming economic barriers to climate action is possible.

Policies that create incentives for businesses to invest in clean energy and reduce their carbon emissions are essential if we are able to overcome the financial obstacles that stand in the way of climate action. This can create a cost for carbon, which would make cleaning exercises more expensive and encourage organizations to put resources into cleaner innovations. Furthermore, states can give endowments or tax incentives to organizations that put resources into clean energy or energy efficiency measures. As demonstrated by Germany and Costa Rica, these policies can also boost economic growth and create jobs.

Social and Cultural Barriers to Action

Global warming and climate change present squeezing challenges that require collective action from individuals, communities, and societies around the world. However, addressing these complex issues is not exclusively a matter of scientific understanding or technological advancements. It also involves navigating social and cultural barriers that influence our attitudes, behaviors, and responses to global warming. Social and cultural barriers encompass a wide range of factors, including public opinion, values, beliefs, social norms, and cultural practices, all of which shape our perceptions and actions in relation to climate change.

Social barriers to action on global warming arise from the intricate exchange of societal dynamics. These barriers can manifest as a lack of awareness, denial, or apathy towards the issue. Public opinion and prevailing social norms may hinder the adoption of sustainable practices or support for effective policies. Overcoming these barriers requires targeted efforts to increase public awareness, foster engagement, and empower communities to take significant action. It involves building consensus, addressing misconceptions, and promoting collective responsibility in tackling global warming.

Cultural barriers, on the other hand, stem from the deeply rooted values, beliefs, and traditions that shape our worldviews. Different cultures may have varying perspectives on the environment, sustainability, and our relationship with nature. Cultural inertia, resistance to change, or conflicts between traditional practices and climate-friendly approaches can impede progress. However, cultural diversity also presents opportunities for creative solutions and alternative perspectives on addressing global warming. By respecting and harnessing cultural values, traditions, and indigenous knowledge, we can advance inclusive and contextually appropriate approaches to climate action.

To address these social and cultural barriers effectively, it is fundamental to cultivate discourse, promote education, and encourage collaboration across diverse stakeholders. Engaging communities, empowering individuals, and recognizing the importance of local contexts can drive meaningful change. Examples from countries like Australia, where community-led initiatives have raised awareness and facilitated grassroots action, or European nations that have implemented ambitious renewable energy policies, showcase the potential for overcoming these barriers. Besides, prioritizing the needs and perspectives of developing countries and vulnerable communities can ensure equitable and inclusive solutions to global warming.

Public perception and awareness play a pivotal part in forming the reaction to climate change. Misinformation, lack of awareness, and skepticism can be boundaries to taking action. For example, (Leiserowitz et al, 2006) found that public misunderstanding of climate science or the perception of uncertainty can hinder support for climate policies. Addressing these boundaries requires effective communication strategies to improve public understanding and awareness of the scientific consensus on climate change.

Cultural values and beliefs also impact demeanors towards environmental issues and can be a barrier to action. Distinctive cultural perspectives on nature, consumption, and obligation may shape individuals' willingness to address climate change. (Kahan et al. 2. , 2011) highlight the significance of cultural cognition in forming people's perception of scientific consensus. Recognizing and engaging with diverse cultural values can cultivate more inclusive and compelling climate action methodologies.

Political ideologies and divisions can hinder climate action as well. Disagreements over the part of government, economic priorities, and climate policy can lead to gridlock and inaction. (McCright & Dunlap, 2011) emphasize the politicization of climate change and its impact on public opinion and policy implementation.

For instance, in the United States, the issue of climate change has become profoundly politicized, with deep divisions along ideological lines. This polarization hinders the execution of comprehensive climate policies and limits public support for climate action. In Australia, a country highly dependent on fossil fuel industries, there is a critical cultural and economic challenge in transitioning to renewable energy. The cultural belief in a strong mining industry and the perceived economic risks associated with renewable energy can impede the necessary policy changes.

In developing countries, social and cultural barriers can be tied to issues of poverty and inequality. For example, in India, where access to reliable energy sources is crucial for economic development, there can be resistance to policies that may limit energy options or increase costs. The focus on immediate economic growth and poverty alleviation can dominate long-term environmental concerns. In contrast, countries like Sweden and Denmark have shown greater societal acceptance and support for climate action due to cultural norms that prioritize sustainability and environmental stewardship.

In Canada, a country heavily dependent on its natural resource industries, there can be resistance to climate policies that may be perceived as threatening economic stability and job security (Sovacool et al., 2020). The cultural attachment to industries like oil and gas extraction can make it challenging to transition to cleaner energy sources.

In Brazil, the Amazon rainforest plays a significant role in the country's cultural identity and economic growth. Balancing the need for economic development with the preservation of the rainforest poses a complex challenge. The cultural values attached to land use, as well as the economic interests of industries like agriculture and logging, can impede endeavors to address deforestation and reduce carbon emissions.

In European countries like Poland, which intensely rely on coal for electricity generation, there can be a strong cultural attachment to the coal industry due to its historical significance and the associated job opportunities. The social acceptance and resistance to change in these communities can pose obstacles to the adoption of renewable energy sources and the phasing out of coal.

In many developing countries, particularly those in sub-Saharan Africa, social and cultural boundaries to action in global warming stem from restricted resources and competing priorities. In countries like Ethiopia, where agriculture is a key sector and rural livelihoods are directly affected by climate change, the focus is often on immediate adaptation measures rather than long-term mitigation efforts (Deressa et al., 2009). Limited access to finance, technology, and education can hinder the adoption of sustainable practices and hinder climate action in these regions.

These examples highlight the diverse social and cultural barriers confronted by different countries in addressing global warming.

In order to effectively address the challenges posed by global warming, it is necessary to adopt a comprehensive strategy that involves the participation of individuals, groups, and organizations, while also taking into consideration the impact of social and cultural factors. A smart approach to address this issue is to focus on education and raising awareness. Educational campaigns, workshops, and school educational modules aimed to increase public awareness of the causes and consequences of global warming. That can equip people with knowledge to make informed decisions while also correcting any misunderstandings. Community involvement is an essential element when it comes to motivating group efforts. Establishing channels for interaction, community-driven campaigns, and citizen-based scientific endeavors can foster a feeling of belonging and empowerment, eliciting active participation in tackling climate change.

Another crucial element is promoting behavioral modifications and shifting societal norms. We can promote the adoption of eco-friendly actions by portraying sustainable practices as attractive and socially acceptable to both individuals and communities. The utilization of peer influence, social marketing initiatives, and social media can serve as powerful means to promote sustainable lifestyles. Being aware and respectful of cultural disparities and sensitivity holds paramount importance in achieving successful efforts towards climate action. Customized solutions that take into account the local environment and incorporate traditional wisdom and expertise should be formulated. Incorporating indigenous communities as partners and involving them in the decision-making process guarantees the usage of culturally fitting methods that draw from their valuable perspectives.

Overcoming boundaries is heavily impacted by policy and government management. Competent governmental policies and regulations can motivate the adoption of sustainable habits, encourage the usage of renewable sources of energy, as well as enforce carbon taxation. Efficient climate action necessitates the presence of policy consistency and strong collaboration among nations at a global level. The use of financial incentives is vital in surpassing economic obstacles. Providing financial assistance in the form of subsidies, tax benefits, and funding opportunities to support renewable energy initiatives and the development of energy-saving technologies could stimulate private sector creativity and investment. By shifting towards a sustainable economy, several employment prospects can be generated and economic progress can be catalyzed all while tackling the issue of global warming.

Success demands collaboration and partnerships. Cooperation among governments, businesses, civil society organizations, and academia can lead to the sharing of expertise, assets, and successful approaches. Developing countries can benefit from the experiences of more developed nations through international cooperation and the exchange of information, which can promote capacity-building. This can foster dynamic collaboration and facilitate progress in these countries. By effectively tackling societal and cultural challenges pertaining to global warming, we can implement these pragmatic solutions and promote a mutual sense of accountability and aspiration toward a sustainable future. Teamwork is necessary to bring about effective and enduring solutions against the challenges presented by global warming. Only through our combined efforts we can achieve meaningful progress.

Psychological Barriers to Action

The complex challenges presented by the psychological barriers that prevent action on climate change call for careful consideration. One perceptible hindrance is the peculiarity of "psychological distancing," in which people see environmental change as a far-off danger eliminated from their nearby lives. This mental detachment can frustrate inspiration and keep people from taking proactive steps.

Besides, the overwhelming complexity and scale of climate change can evoke feelings of frailty and despair, making it difficult for individuals to envision its impact. Also, cognitive biases, such as the tendency to seek information that confirms pre-existing beliefs or the unwarranted optimism that others will address the issue, can create resistance to accepting the urgency of climate change. Understanding and addressing these psychological barriers is crucial in fostering individual and collective action toward mitigating climate change.

Psychological barriers play a significant role in impeding progress toward addressing environmental issues. The limitations that stem from human cognition, emotion, and behavior can impact people's attitudes, convictions, and willingness to take action. The fact that climate change is often viewed as a remote and intangible concern hinders individuals from feeling a tangible sense of involvement or being inspired to be proactive (Spence et al., 2012).

People's affinity to engage in cognitive predispositions like persuaded thinking and affirmation inclination is another psychological barrier. According to (Kahan et al. 2. , 2012) individuals frequently reject or dismiss evidence that challenges their views on climate change. As a result, they look for information that supports their pre-existing beliefs and values. This mental inclination can support existing convictions and make it try to change perspectives or progress environmental action

Emotions play a significant role in shaping how people respond to alterations in their surroundings. The concern could result in a range of emotions, including a sense of vulnerability, remorse, and anxiety. According to (Clayton et al., 2015), the intense emotions that arise from a significant problem can be difficult to handle, leading individuals to react tentatively or avoid certain behaviors as they try to cope with the deep distress.

Individuals' views and actions on climate change are also influenced by social and cultural factors. Individuals' perceptions of whether climate action is socially desirable or necessary can be influenced by cultural values, social norms, and peer pressure. Climate action can be facilitated or hampered by the influence of social groups and institutions (Feldman et al., 2014).

Aside from emotional and cognitive biases, there are additional psychological obstacles that hinder action toward addressing climate change. Another significant psychological hurdle is the uniqueness of "perceived behavioral control," which refers to individuals' beliefs regarding their ability to effectively take action to address climate change. According to (Stern, 2000) individuals' willingness to adopt environmentally-friendly behaviors may decrease if they doubt the effectiveness of their actions or perceive themselves as lacking the necessary resources or knowledge to make a positive impact.

In addition, barriers caused by "temporal discounting," or prioritizing short-term benefits over long-term ones, frequently hinder individuals. According to (Milfont & Duckitt, 2010), people may struggle to prioritize climate change mitigation when confronted with more immediate issues and benefits.

Social factors also shape psychological barriers to taking action on environmental change. People's perceptions of and responses to environmental issues are influenced by cultural worldviews, values, and ideologies. According to (Milfont & Sibley, 2014), individualistic cultures, for instance, maybe more resistant to collective action and environmental regulations. These cultures place an emphasis on personal freedom and economic expansion.

Additionally, attitudes toward climate change and the perceived importance of addressing it can be influenced by cultural differences in beliefs about the relationship between humans and nature.

To overcome the psychological barriers that inhibit action towards addressing climate change, it is necessary to put into effect practical solutions that are efficient. A crucial approach is utilizing tailored messaging and communication tactics. Crafting targeted messages that take into account the unique values, beliefs, and identities of different audiences can effectively counteract cognitive biases and cultivate favorable perceptions of climate action (Nisbet & Myers, 2007). Highlighting the practical and observable advantages of embracing environmentally-friendly habits, such as financial benefits or enhanced well-being, can inspire people to make a change (Bamberg & Möser, 2007).

Overcoming psychological hurdles greatly depends on the effectiveness of education and awareness initiatives. Giving extensive and easily comprehensible knowledge about what triggers climate change, its consequences, and feasible remedies can amplify comprehension and authorize individuals in making educated decisions (Hines et al., 1986). Educating children about climate change during their formative years, incorporating related topics into school syllabi, and providing educational opportunities for adults can encourage sustainable practices in the long run (Schultz et al., 2005).

Social conventions and the influence of peers have a considerable impact on individual actions. Encouraging individuals to adopt climate-friendly behaviors can be achieved by emphasizing positive social norms and the actions of role models who already engage in such behaviors (Nolan et al., 2008). Community-led programs that promote joint efforts and form supportive relationships have the potential to enhance individuals' confidence in their ability to make a difference and cultivate a social setting that encourages sustainable conduct.

Establishing supportive structures and enacting policy measures play a vital role in surmounting psychological hurdles. To overcome obstacles linked to affordability and availability, providing incentives like monetary rewards or subsidies that promote the adoption of renewable energy technologies and energy-saving practices can be effective (Abrahamse & Steg, 2013). The introduction of guidelines and norms that encourage eco-friendly actions in various sectors such as transportation, buildings, and industries can influence people's decisions and lead to a significant transformation in society.

Participatory processes involving a variety of stakeholders can effectively overcome psychological obstacles. Incorporating the perspectives and suggestions of people and groups in decision-making procedures, and facilitating authentic participation, can augment the sense of ownership and mutual accountability. It is crucial to establish cooperation among governments, corporations, educational institutions, and civil society groups to create and execute successful climate action plans (Patterson et al., 2017).

Although the solutions presented can serve as a starting point, it is crucial to acknowledge that tackling psychological obstacles involves a varied approach that recognizes the distinct attributes of distinct groups, cultural circumstances, and financial aspects. It is crucial to regularly conduct research and assessment of interventions in order to pinpoint and improve techniques that effectively overcome psychological obstacles and encourage lasting modifications in behavior.

Technological Barriers to Action

The significance of technology cannot be underestimated when it comes to tackling the issue of global climate change. It possesses the solution to liberate inventive solutions and facilitate the shift towards a lasting future. Despite the efforts, technological limitations pose significant obstacles that hinder our advancement. The obstacles to incorporating renewable energy systems within current infrastructure are multifaceted and include affordability and accessibility of sustainable technologies, as well as compatibility and integration issues. To surmount these obstacles successfully, we must encourage cooperation, advance investigation and innovation, and establish favorable regulations and motivation.

Overcoming technological barriers presently poses substantial difficulties in implementing efficient measures to address climate change. A major obstacle lies in the accessibility and affordability of environmentally friendly technologies. Renewable energy methods, such as wind turbines and solar panels, have become more economical lately. Nevertheless, they necessitate an initial investment that could deter individuals, businesses, and governments, particularly in underdeveloped nations. Furthermore, the insufficient infrastructure to store and distribute renewable energy can hinder its extensive implementation (Chu & Majumdar, 2012). These barriers highlight the importance of regulations and motivators that lower the expenses of eco-friendly innovations and simplify their implementation and assimilation into current energy structures.

The integration and compatibility of renewable energy systems with current infrastructure pose another barrier to taking action on climate change. Replacing traditional fossil fuel energy sources with renewable sources involves major transformations in the production, distribution, and utilization of energy. The process of transitioning to renewable energy sources comes with its own set of difficulties which include the need to adjust electrical grids to suit the variability of renewable energy, come up with storage solutions that guarantee reliability and upgrade buildings and transportation systems to make them more energy-efficient. The hurdles pertaining to compatibility and integration necessitate thorough comprehensive planning, coordination, and substantial financial commitment in research and development to surmount technological drawbacks and ensure a seamless shift towards a low-carbon economic system.

The speed at which technology advances is imperative in overcoming technological barriers in addressing climate change. Developments in technology including enhanced solar panels, energy storage systems on a large scale, and the ability to capture and store carbon have the ability to bring about a major change in the energy industry and bring down the amount of greenhouse gas discharged. In order to fully exploit the benefits of these technological upgrades, it is imperative to allocate more resources towards research and development. The allocation of resources for fundamental investigations and partnerships among academic institutions, businesses, and the government for the conversion of scientific breakthroughs into feasible answers are incorporated in this. Moreover, it is necessary to tackle matters related to intellectual property rights and the transfer of technology in order to guarantee access to eco-friendly technologies for all nations, especially those requiring sustainable development remedies.

It is essential to tackle the technological challenges associated with addressing climate change is the prioritization of research and development endeavors aimed at boosting technological advancement. It is crucial for governments, research institutions, and private sector organizations to escalate their investments in clean energy research, development, and demonstration initiatives. One strategy for progress is to allocate resources towards the development of renewable energy technologies, energy storage systems, and carbon capture and storage techniques (Grubler et al., 2018). To promote creativity and backing up technical advancements, we can expedite the creation of affordable and widely adaptable sustainable energy alternatives.

In order to effectively tackle technological barriers, it is crucial to establish collaboration among the various parties involved. Collaborations between the public and private sectors can promote the transfer of knowledge, the sharing of resources, and cooperation in research endeavors. Collaboration can be encouraged by governments through the creation of networks, clusters, and partnerships between industries and academic institutions that are dedicated to developing environmentally friendly and sustainable technologies. Collaborative efforts that combine varied skills and resources can speed up the creation and implementation of groundbreaking technologies, facilitating the shift towards an eco-friendly economy.

It is essential to prioritize the promotion of technology transfer and capacity building, especially for developing nations that could encounter more significant obstacles in terms of technology. Developed nations can assist in the transfer of technology by extending financial aid, specialized knowledge, and educational courses to enable underdeveloped countries to embrace and execute eco-friendly energy solutions (IPCC, 2014). An effective approach to aiding developing nations in acquiring and implementing eco-friendly technologies is possible by employing strategies like the Green Climate Fund and Technology Mechanism, both of which are established within the UNFCCC framework (UNFCCC).

Having policy support and regulatory frameworks plays a pivotal role in surmounting technological barriers. The suggestion made by the IEA (2020) is for governments to introduce measures that encourage the usage of eco-friendly technologies, for instance, by providing financial benefits such as feed-in tariffs, tax exemptions, and subsidies for clean energy initiatives. Moreover, regulations have the potential to incentivize advancements in energy efficiency, advocate for the adoption of eco-friendly modes of transport, and ensure strict adherence to targets for reducing emissions. Having unambiguous and consistent policies in place can create a predictable environment for the market, drawing in private sector investments while stimulating growth and innovation in the clean energy sectors.

Smart education and increased awareness hold the solution to surmounting technological barriers faced by both individuals and communities. Spreading awareness through public outreach programs, educational campaigns, and capacity-building initiatives can increase understanding of clean technologies, their advantages, and how people can contribute to adopting eco-friendly habits. By equipping people with knowledge and expertise, we can cultivate a mentality of sustainability and generate a desire for eco-friendly solutions, thereby promoting greater usage and integration of clean technologies in day-to-day activities.

Chapter 11

Real-world Insights into Climate Change Solutions

The global effects of climate change are already taking place, making it a significant challenge of our era. In light of the pressing need to tackle this issue, it's vital to draw inspiration and guidance from practical examples and success stories. In this chapter, we will go through numerous case studies that offer us valuable perspectives on tackling climate change in various settings.

Every instance of analysis provides valuable insights into the hands-on usage of tactics and methodologies directed towards reducing the impacts of climate change and adapting to its effects. These actual occurrences provide insights into the potential, hindrances, and knowledge gained as societies, groups, and states endeavor to establish a sustainable and adaptive future.

The case studies shared in this chapter are not just abstract ideas but practical illustrations of practical solutions that have had a discernible impact in the real world. By means of these stories, we delve into the difficulties confronted by individuals and groups, the methods utilized to overcome obstacles, and the substantial changes accomplished. Thoroughly analyzing these narratives provides us with a greater comprehension of how social, economic, and environmental elements intertwine in the quest for achieving sustainability.

Furthermore, these case studies not only highlight success stories but also provide insight into the obstacles and constraints faced throughout the journey. It is important to acknowledge that there are obstacles to overcome in the pursuit of enacting solutions for climate change. Innovative and persistent efforts are often necessary to overcome the challenges presented by scarce resources, political intricacies, and technological obstacles.

Nevertheless, if we comprehend and tackle these impediments, we have the opportunity to gain insights from accomplishments and shortcomings and endeavor to incessantly enhance our combined efforts to combat climate change.

This chapter serves as evidence that climate change cannot be addressed with a universal solution. Instead, it accentuates the multitude of methods, plans, and actions that can be customized to suit individual situations and obstacles. There are many different ways that both individuals and large organizations can contribute to efforts to mitigate and adapt to climate change, ranging from small community-based projects to national-level policies.

The following insights urge us to implement strategies for reducing our carbon footprints and ensuring a sustainable future.

Natural methods for addressing climate change show great potential for reducing greenhouse gas emissions and preserving the environment through land conservation, restoration, and improved management, all of which increase carbon storage. Through the utilization of nature's capabilities, natural approaches to managing the environment can significantly contribute to carbon sequestration and minimize the effects of climate change. (The Nature Conservancy, 2017)

It is crucial to rely on scientific solutions to achieve a speedy reduction of carbon emissions and assist communities in adapting to the effects of climate change. These methods require exhaustive scientific studies and technological progress that aid the growth of green energy resources, eco-friendly infrastructure, and weather-resistant structures. Science-based solutions, which rely on scientific knowledge and evidence-based approaches, offer efficient strategies for tackling the complications posed by climate change (Royal Society, 2021).

Dealing with climate change involves acknowledging and emphasizing the importance of personal actions. Individuals can positively impact sustainability and diminish greenhouse gas emissions by selecting energy sources, transportation modes, and food intake wisely. The consequences of individual actions become much more significant when people come together to take collective action. Individuals have the ability to enact significant change and pave the way for a more sustainable future by collaborating through community initiatives, advocacy campaigns, and grassroots movements (Greenpeace).

Smart technological solutions play a crucial role in the efforts towards mitigating and adapting to climate change. Advancements in sustainable energy technologies, storage solutions for energy, and the storage of carbon are essential components for achieving a shift towards an economy with fewer emissions. New technological developments like durable electric vehicle batteries, solutions based on hydrogen, and carbon capture and storage can bring a revolutionary change to energy systems and drastically decrease greenhouse gas emissions (NRDC, 2022).

Geoengineering is an option to be utilized only in dire circumstances and involves innovative methods to confront the issues of climate change. Some of the actions that can be taken involve methods such as obstructing sunlight or eliminating the presence of gases that contribute to the greenhouse effect. Although they are subject to much debate and scrutiny, techniques for geoengineering have been investigated as possible measures for reducing the effects of climate change. (Scientific American, 2007)

Case Studies of Successful Implementation of Natural Climate Solutions in Different Regions

Innovative and effective measures are necessary to counteract the detrimental impacts of climate change. In this part, we delve into practical instances of climate solutions that have effectively tackled the climate crisis and produced noticeable results.

An outstanding instance can be seen in Germany's shift towards sustainable energy sources. The nation has made impressive progress in the gradual elimination of traditional fuel sources and in shifting towards an economy based on lower levels of carbon emissions. The drive towards the Energiewende, or energy transition, has necessitated a repertoire of measures, including policies, incentives, and investments, to facilitate the growth and implementation of sustainable energy technologies. Germany's dedication to green energy has led to a significant upsurge in the proportion of renewable sources in its energy blend. As of 2020, renewable energy accounted for more than 40% of the country's electricity production. The switch to this new system has brought about not just a decrease in the release of greenhouse gases but has also led to the generation of employment opportunities, sparked new ideas and inventions, and boosted the security of our energy resources.

The implementation of carbon pricing mechanisms has proven to be an effective solution to address climate issues. Carbon pricing, which involves implementing either a carbon tax or a cap-and-trade mechanism, offers a financial motivation to limit the release of greenhouse gases into the atmosphere. A distinctive illustration is the implementation of the carbon pricing system in British Columbia, Canada. In 2008, the region unveiled a carbon tax that aimed to balance out the generated revenue, and the tax has been gradually raised over time, according to the British Columbia Ministry of Finance. Through the implementation of the carbon tax, both individuals and businesses have been motivated to decrease their carbon footprint, leading to a substantial drop in per-person emissions, stated by the British Columbia Ministry of Finance. This particular study showcases the success of utilizing market-based approaches to encourage a reduction in emissions while also creating funds for sustainable projects.

Local efforts driven by the community have exhibited effectiveness in tackling climate change from the ground up. An instance of this is the widespread Transition Town movement that originated in Totnes, UK. Transition towns are localized movements driven by the community to enhance resilience and diminish carbon emissions through their own efforts and initiatives. These programs encompass a range of measures, including advocating for the use of renewable energy sources, introducing eco-friendly transportation alternatives, and supporting localized food cultivation. Transition towns have provided communities with the ability to manage their own energy usage and establish practices that are environmentally sustainable, resulting in a decrease in emissions and a greater ability for the community to withstand adversity. (Hopkins, 2008).

Nature-based solutions have proven to be effective methods for mitigating climate change. Preserving and restoring forests is vital in the effort to store carbon dioxide and maintain biodiversity. Costa Rica's implementation of the REDD+ program is a prime illustration of the effective use of nature-based solutions. By employing a variety of tactics, including offering monetary benefits, implementing land-use regulations, and engaging citizens, Costa Rica has effectively lowered rates of deforestation and improved the amount of forested land available. By adopting this method, we are not only reducing the impact of climate change but also supporting the preservation of ecosystems and promoting sustainable development.

The successful adoption of energy efficiency programs is another noteworthy demonstration of effective climate solutions. The emphasis of energy efficiency measures is to decrease the usage of energy and enhance the efficacy of energy utilization in various domains like structures, factory outcomes, and conveyance. A noteworthy instance is Denmark's endeavors toward achieving higher energy efficiency. By using a mix of governmental assistance, monetary bonuses, and public education efforts, Denmark has accomplished impressive enhancements in energy efficiency across diverse domains. The nation's dedication to enhancing energy efficiency has yielded positive outcomes, including a decline in energy consumption, reduced greenhouse gas emissions, and financial benefits for households and companies. The case of Denmark's triumph in energy efficiency aptly illustrates the significance of well-rounded protocols and efficient execution as effective means to attain notable reductions in emissions.

Moreover, sustainable farming techniques present encouraging prospects for addressing climate change alongside energy-based resolutions. The technique known as the System of Rice Intensification (SRI) is an excellent instance of an agricultural approach that is intelligent and adaptive to the changing climate. SRI refers to a collection of techniques that enhance the cultivation of rice by reducing water consumption and greenhouse gas emissions as well as increasing crop production. The implementation of SRI techniques in rice farming has demonstrated considerable potential for reducing methane discharge, preserving water supplies, and improving food stability. The utilization of SRI techniques in diverse nations like India and Madagascar has provided evidence of the effectiveness of resilient farming methods in mitigating agricultural emissions.

Successful conservation efforts have been observed in Indonesia through the implementation of the Rimba Raya Biodiversity Reserve, a REDD+ initiative that safeguards and rehabilitates peat swamp woodlands. This program not only aids in reducing climate change but also offers advantages to the nearby population (Frontiersin.org). The Jari Pará Forest Conservation Project in Brazil has succeeded in safeguarding and rehabilitating forests while offering benefits to the surrounding community, making it a prosperous REDD+ initiative (Nature4Climate.org).

A report called Natural Climate Solutions for the United States has been released, which outlines several interventions related to conservation, restoration, and land management that can help reduce the impact of climate change in the country. Several methods, such as reforestation, afforestation, and soil carbon sequestration, are employed to mitigate climate change (Science.org). The 30x30 Forests, Food, and Land Challenge is a global effort that seeks to address climate change by conserving, restoring, and enhancing the management of forests, food systems, and other natural lands (NWF).

According to American University, the Payment for Ecosystem Services initiative in Mexico is a successful approach that encourages landowners to safeguard and rehabilitate forests, resulting in advantages for nearby populations. The Agroforestry for Livelihoods Improvement project encourages the use of agroforestry methods in India to improve soil quality, capture more carbon, and create extra sources of income for farmers (IOP).

In addition, there are possibilities for sustainable transportation options in the mobility sector. Electric cars are becoming increasingly popular as a viable substitute for conventional vehicles that rely on internal combustion engines. Norway has become a convincing model for the promotion of electric vehicle adoption. The nation has established a comprehensive program of perks that involves substantial monetary benefits, toll exemptions, and priority entry to bus lanes. Norway's successful transition to electric transportation highlights the critical role that encouraging policies, infrastructure expansion, and financial motivation play in accelerating this process.

These examples showcase the effective application of natural climate solutions across various regions, highlighting the potential benefits of sustainable practices in addressing climate change and promoting the well-being of both the environment and the surrounding communities.

Collaboration and agreements between nations are essential to tackling the issue of climate change at a global level. The international climate collaboration achieved a major milestone with the adoption of the Paris Agreement in 2015. The UNFCCC established an agreement with the goal of restricting the increase of the Earth's temperature to less than 2 degrees Celsius, with the added objective of striving to keep it below 1.5 degrees Celsius. In 2015, the UNFCCC stated that the Paris Agreement has inspired nations globally to establish objectives for lowering emissions, bolstering their ability to cope with the effects of climate change, and encouraging lasting growth. The dedication of nations to this common cause promotes teamwork, information exchange, and joint initiatives, showcasing the significance of global partnership in attaining environmentally friendly objectives.

Challenges Faced During the Implementation of Natural Climate Solutions

Numerous obstacles arise when executing natural climate solutions. Engaging indigenous communities and local populations poses a major obstacle (Ingrid et al., 2022). It is essential to engage these stakeholders since their expertise and involvement are crucial factors in achieving success in implementing natural climate solutions. Furthermore, the prosperous implementation of methods that rely on nature is contingent upon the socio-ecological and environmental circumstances (Ellezelle et al., 2022). Every locality has its own set of situations, necessitating individualized techniques and deliberations.

Evaluating solutions that involve natural surroundings and effectively managing the balance between advantages and disadvantages are crucial tasks. Quantifying the effectiveness of natural climate solutions holds great significance in comprehending their potential impact (JOSEPH E et al., 2018). Through the precise evaluation of their capabilities, those in charge of decision-making can make informed decisions and efficiently distribute resources. In addition, it is recommended to incorporate nature-based strategies alongside other approaches, such as reducing greenhouse gas emissions and implementing engineered carbon removal techniques, to create an all-encompassing plan for addressing climate change (American University)

Encountering hindrances is also a possibility when trying to put into practice regulations that encourage landowners to engage in conservation and restoration endeavors (Nature4Climate.org)

Challenges exist that can impede the effective implementation of natural climate solutions as seen in the case studies. The insufficient collaboration and communication among various government departments may obstruct the successful execution of climate measures and impede the inclusion of natural climate solutions into wider plans (Giles, 2021).

The absence of well-defined advantages poses an obstacle in integrating the implementation of nature-oriented solutions into mainstream practices. The EPA Climate Change Interest Group acknowledges the difficulty and emphasizes the significance of effectively communicating the advantages of natural climate solutions in order to gain backing and dedication from stakeholders (European Commission, 2020). It can be difficult to obtain enough support and resources to put a plan into action if the advantages are unclear or not effectively conveyed.

Much like the previously discussed obstacles, the social, ecological, and environmental circumstances are essential in determining the effectiveness of using nature-based methods to combat climate change. The appropriateness and efficiency of these remedies may differ depending on particular socio-ecological and environmental circumstances. Designing and implementing natural climate solutions should take into account multiple factors, including but not limited to land use history, biodiversity, and the provision of ecosystem services (Lewis et al., 2020).

It is essential to involve indigenous communities and locals in order to effectively execute natural climate solutions. Despite its potential benefits, it can present difficulties as a result of diverse viewpoints, complications related to land ownership, and past inequities. To ensure that all stakeholders participate meaningfully, their rights and traditional knowledge should be respected, and benefits should be shared equitably, it is important to make concerted efforts (Ingrid Schulte et al., 2021).

The notion that nature-based solutions are not effective enough can hinder their implementation. In South Korea, there were concerns that nature-oriented methods for controlling flood hazards might not be sufficient, which could impede their widespread implementation. To overcome this obstacle, it is vital to enhance comprehension, communication, and demonstrations based on evidence of the efficacy of natural climate solutions in addressing these perceptions (Kim et al., 2021).

The intricate and multifaceted aspects of carrying out natural climate solutions are emphasized by these difficulties. If the challenges are dealt with proficiently, nature-based solutions have the potential to be utilized to the fullest extent in curbing climate change.

Real-world Examples of Adaptation and Resilience

The planet is currently encountering changes in mean temperature, variations in the timing of seasons, an escalation in the instances of severe weather phenomena, and gradual onset occurrences. The longer we procrastinate in addressing climate change, the more complicated and costly it will be to adapt to the accelerated environmental changes.

Adaptation and resilience denote modifications made in natural, societal, or financial frameworks as a reaction to foreseeable or present climate-related triggers and their consequences. This pertains to alterations in procedures, methods, and frameworks aimed at mitigating possible negative effects or capitalizing on benefits related to variations in climate patterns. Essentially, nations and societies must devise and execute measures to address the present and future effects of climate change through adaptation methods. We will provide instances from actual settings that demonstrate the effective application of adaptation and resilience measures across various areas.

The strategies used for adaptation can vary greatly based on the specific circumstances of a community, business, organization, country or region. Adaptation methods cannot be applied universally, as they range from constructing flood barriers and implementing timely alerts for hurricanes, to cultivating drought-tolerant crops and modifying communication networks, company procedures, and governmental regulations. Numerous countries and groups are presently implementing measures to develop durable societies and economies.

The Netherlands is famed for its inventive tactics towards water governance and assimilation. The Delta Works comprises a range of expansive infrastructure initiatives designed to safeguard the nation from floods and surging seawater levels. This involves building dams, embankments, and protective barriers against storm surges, as well as adopting innovative methods for managing water resources. The steps taken have notably lessened the likelihood of flood occurrences and bolstered the nation's ability to withstand the effects of climate change (Ministry of Infrastructure and Water Management).

The biggest connected mangrove forest on the planet is the Sundarbans, located in Bangladesh and India. It acts as a natural shield from the damaging impact of storm surges and rising sea levels, safeguarding the welfare of the coastal communities. Due to the crucial role of the Sundarbans in enhancing climate resilience, diverse measures have been taken to adapt, such as community-led mangrove rehabilitation schemes, sustainable income-generating initiatives, and alert systems for cyclones. The measures taken have improved the resilience of nearby communities and their capability to endure climatic dangers (UNDP Bangladesh).

The Great Barrier Reef, which is a renowned UNESCO World Heritage destination, is endangered by climate change, involving challenges such as coral bleaching and ocean acidification. Australia has taken a number of measures to adjust and safeguard this renowned ecosystem in order to maintain and protect it. There are several things that can be done to improve the condition of coral reefs such as enhancing the quality of water to alleviate pressure on the corals, enforcing rigorous fishing guidelines, and creating protected zones in the ocean. Furthermore, endeavors are underway to conduct studies and surveillance initiatives aimed at achieving a more comprehensive comprehension of the Great Barrier Reef's endurance capabilities and to provide invaluable information that can aid in the formulation of effective strategies for future adjustments (Great Barrier Reef Marine Park Authority).

Copenhagen has gained considerable acclaim for its initiatives to adapt and endure as an eco-friendly and resilient municipality amid the impact of climate change. The metropolis has put into effect multiple initiatives to cope with the increasing levels of water in the ocean, which involve building barricades to avoid floods and upgrading the systems for managing stormwater.

Copenhagen has given significant importance to sustainable transportation, with a focus on developing cycling infrastructure and allocating resources towards public transportation. The efforts undertaken have not only enhanced the city's ability to withstand challenges but also boosted the standard of living for its inhabitants (City of Copenhagen).

The Mesoamerican Reef System, which is situated in Mexico, Belize, Guatemala, and Honduras, is the world's second-largest coral reef. In an effort to safeguard the valuable marine ecosystem that is ecologically diverse and economically significant, these nations have joined forces through the Mesoamerican Reef Tourism Initiative (MARTI). MARTI's aim is to enhance climate endurance through sustainable tourism techniques, tracking of coral reefs, and involving the community. These countries are striving for strong adaptation and sustainability by cultivating responsible tourism practices and safeguarding the natural resources of the reef (The Nature Conservancy).

Prek Toal, a village that floats in the Tonle Sap Biosphere Reserve, confronts a host of climate change issues such as elevated flooding and variations in water levels. The community has developed ingenious ways such as cultivating floating gardens and expanding fish farming to cope with changes and increase their ability to withstand tough times. By adopting these techniques, the community can cultivate agriculture and breed aquatic animals in accordance with the dynamically evolving surroundings. Prek Toal's floating village is an exemplary model of how communities can take charge of their adaptation to environmental changes and implement sustainable practices to boost their resilience (United Nations Development Programme).

The Disaster Mitigation and Adaptation Fund (DMAF) in Canada facilitates the management of natural hazard risks such as floods, wildfires, and droughts within communities through investments in both natural and man-made infrastructure. The Global Centre for Adaptation states that the DMAF offers financial support to initiatives aimed at bolstering the capacity of communities to withstand and recover from disasters, including the construction of flood-proof facilities, rehabilitation of natural habitats, and establishment of advance notification mechanisms.

To improve its resistance to heavy rainfall and decrease the likelihood of floods, the city is taking actions like afforesting, reviving wetlands, and enhancing drainage systems (United Nations).

The UNEP has recently issued guidelines detailing measures for constructing climate-resilient buildings and green spaces. These recommendations focus on utilizing nature-based solutions that incorporate green roofs, urban forests, and permeable surfaces as effective measures to reduce the impact of climate risks and improve the city's resilience.

The World Bank is financing a project in Bangladesh that aims to construct homes that are resistant to climate-related challenges. These resilient houses are made from materials that can withstand natural disasters and come equipped with elevated water tanks. These residences are constructed to endure cyclones, flooding, and other perils associated with weather patterns. The plan comprises of initiatives aimed at promoting disaster readiness and reducing hazards in the community, thus enhancing the endurance of disadvantaged neighborhoods as well (World Bank).

The Upper West region of Ghana has implemented an early warning system that relies on remote sensing technology to identify any alterations in water levels. By doing so, the Upper West Regional Coordinating Council (URC) can take proactive measures and alert the inhabitants of two districts about possible flooding. The system imparts prompt information that enables communities to take appropriate measures and evacuate promptly, minimizing the threat to lives and property (Global Centre for Adaptation).

The movable flood barrier known as the Thames Barrier serves to safeguard London against tidal surges that may occur within the River Thames. The intention behind the barrier is to protect against flooding during extreme tides and surges caused by storms, ensuring that crucial infrastructure is resilient and the city is shielded from the consequences of rising sea levels and the adverse effects of climate change.

Governments have the potential to aid in adaptation efforts by enhancing infrastructure, reevaluating land usage policies, safeguarding vital ecosystems, and forming a strong legal and institutional structure. The World Bank highlights the significance of taking these measures in order to bolster the ability of communities to withstand adversity and promote ecological stability amidst climate change.

Infrastructure that is able to withstand extreme climate impacts, such as roads, bridges, and power lines, is considered to be climate-resilient. One can promote investments in infrastructure that can withstand climate changes by implementing various methods such as enforcing building codes, utilizing vulnerability maps in spatial planning, and effectively communicating climate risks, forecasts, and indeterminate factors to the private sector. The integration of resilient aspects into infrastructure planning and design enables communities to diminish vulnerabilities and adjust to climatic changes, mentioned by UNEP).

To achieve successful adaptation and resilience, it is crucial for all parties to play an active and sustained role, including governments, local communities, varied organizations, civil society, and other relevant actors. Effective management of knowledge is also necessary in this process. The participants in the UNFCCC and the Paris Agreement acknowledge that adaptation poses a worldwide issue that has varying levels of influence, ranging from local to international scales.

Being able to adapt and bounce back is an essential element of the sustainable worldwide approach to addressing climate change, with the ultimate aim of safeguarding individuals, their means of living, and the environment. Both parties recognize that adaptation strategies should prioritize a nation-led, inclusive, and transparent approach that takes into account the needs of vulnerable individuals, communities, and ecosystems, with particular emphasis on gender-responsive measures. The integration of adaptation into socioeconomic and environmental policies and actions should take into consideration the most reliable scientific information and, where applicable, the traditional knowledge, indigenous peoples' knowledge, and local knowledge systems.

Chapter 12

Conclusion

Immediate actions need to be taken to address the notable hurdles presented by climate change and the resulting global warming of our planet. In our book, we have delved into the diverse aspects of climate change and offer practical ideas for reducing its impact on our planet.

The scientific evidence of climate change has been thoroughly explored in this book, along with the subsequent effects on both ecological and human communities. Our book explores various dimensions of climate change and presents feasible strategies to mitigate its adverse effects on our environment.

To discover sustainable energy alternatives, we analyzed the feasibility of solar, wind, and hydropower as potential substitutes for non-renewable fossil fuels. The effectiveness of strategies centered around nature, including ecosystem restoration, reforestation, and sustainable land management, in carbon sequestration and preserving biodiversity has been demonstrated by the efforts to explore natural climate solutions.

The advancement of these initiatives has been greatly influenced by the active participation of global organizations like the United Nations Environment Program, along with the dedication of governments and communities all over the world. Addressing the difficulties brought about by climate change requires an all-encompassing approach that includes vital factors like infrastructure that is resilient to climate, systems of early warning, and the integration of solutions based on nature into urban planning.

By acknowledging the potential of renewable energy sources and dedicating resources towards their advancement, we can shift towards a viable energy future that lessens our carbon footprint. By adopting natural climate solutions like sustainable land management and reforestation, it's possible to not only sequester carbon but also safeguard crucial ecosystems and enrich biodiversity. Highlighting the interdependence between the environment, society, and climate, these approaches emphasize the importance of taking a comprehensive approach to tackle climate change.

The book presents examples of viable adaptation and resilience initiatives, indicating that it is feasible to achieve transformative change. It is important to recognize that additional action is required to expand and duplicate these endeavors to adequately address the scale of the problem.

We need to fundamentally change our actions, rules, and cultural values in order to tackle the issue of climate change. Collaborative dedication towards sustainable habits, conscientious usage, and careful environmental management is required. By integrating climate concerns into every facet of our existence, ranging from city design to farming to company activities, we can establish a stronger and more environmentally-friendly future.

It is crucial to recognize that the battle against climate change encompasses more than just preserving the natural world. Rather, it is about securing the welfare and prospects of mankind. Underprivileged societies, particularly in less-developed nations, are the most affected by the consequences of climate change. As such, it is crucial that we give utmost importance to fairness, equal opportunities, and diversity in our endeavors to address climate change.

The measures illustrated in this book must not be seen as independent undertakings, but need to be integrated into a wider global response. Meaningful change can be accomplished only through collaboration between governments, stakeholders, and individuals. Through collaborative efforts, we can shift towards an economy with reduced carbon emissions, shield susceptible communities, and ensure the preservation of our planet for future generations.

The Urgent Need for Action

It is crucial to emphasize the necessity of urgent action against climate change. There is abundant and conclusive scientific research indicating that the planet's climate is rapidly heating up, largely as a result of human actions such as burning fossil fuels, industrial operations, and deforestation. The effects of climate change are currently being experienced across the globe, manifesting as elevated temperatures, reduced ice caps, heightened occurrences of extreme weather and more serious impacts on natural habitats and species diversity.

Reliable scientific studies, incorporating the findings of the Intergovernmental Panel on Climate Change (IPCC), consistently highlight the critical need to reduce greenhouse gas emissions and adapt to the changing climate by taking prompt and decisive measures. The longer we wait to take action, the more severe the damage will be and the harder it will be to control global warming within safe boundaries.

Prompt action to address climate change is crucial because it disproportionately affects vulnerable communities, especially those in less developed countries and marginalized societies. These communities frequently experience restricted resources and are at greater risk to the impacts of climate change. This places them in a vulnerable position, leading to issues such as inadequate access to food and water, forced relocation, and negative health consequences. To ensure equity in the climate and secure the rights and well-being of all individuals, no one can be left out and immediate and determined steps are necessary.

The urgency to take immediate action is also supported by strong economic reasoning. The expenses of not taking action are much greater than the expenses needed for measures of mitigation and adaptation. According to the World Bank, the expenses of adjusting to the impacts of climate change could potentially climb up to $140-$300 billion every year by 2030, with a possibility of soaring to $280-$500 billion per year by 2050. On the flip side, implementing proactive measures in the present could result in substantial economic advantages, such as the generation of environmentally-friendly employment opportunities, advancements in sustainable technologies, and enhanced energy conservation.

The pressing requirement for action can only be met with the joint collaboration and determination of leaders and nations across the globe. Almost every nation in the world has signed the Paris Agreement, which outlines a pathway for worldwide cooperation aimed at restricting global warming to under 2 degrees Celsius, with additional efforts in place to keep it below 1. 5 Achieving the objectives outlined in the Paris Agreement necessitates an elevated and swifter dedication from all countries to mitigate emissions and assist susceptible nations in adjusting to the effects of climate change.

Combating climate change necessitates a combined and exhaustive reaction involving all sectors, including governments, enterprises, societies, and individuals. The problem at hand can no longer be considered future generations' responsibility as it is now an urgent matter that requires prompt action. The chance to restrict the rise in global temperatures and stave off disastrous outcomes is swiftly diminishing. Delaying action on climate change will only increase the difficulty and expense of reducing its effects and adjusting to them.

The need for immediate climate action is accentuated by the idea of tipping points, referring to crucial limits that, once exceeded, could trigger irreversible and sudden shifts within the Earth's climate system. As an example, if the Greenland and West Antarctic ice sheets were to melt, it could result in a noteworthy increase in sea levels, which would lead to the displacement of millions of individuals and the destruction of cities situated along the coast. The urgency to take immediate action and prevent surpassing the limits of the Earth's equilibrium is evident during the critical stages of reaching a tipping point.

Ensuring public awareness and motivation towards combating climate change is crucial. Each person possesses the ability to effect change by consciously making thoughtful decisions and actions in their everyday lives. By embracing sustainable methods, lessening our impact on the environment, and supporting policies that promote climate preservation, we play a crucial part in the joint endeavor to tackle this worldwide issue. Education and awareness initiatives are essential in promoting environmental responsibility and empowering individuals to take proactive steps towards improving the environment.

It is imperative that we understand that the pressing requirement for response extends beyond just limiting carbon emissions. It is equally important to build resilience and adapt to the impacts of climate change. Smart measures will be taken to ensure the security of communities at high risk, building infrastructure that can withstand climate-related impacts, exploring alternative sources for energy and water, and improving capacities for response and preparedness against disasters. By giving adaptation a greater importance, we can reduce the dangers associated with climate change and guarantee the sustainable welfare of societies and environments in the long run.

Global efforts of collaboration and cooperation are essential in addressing the challenges posed by climate change. This challenge cannot be tackled by any one nation in isolation. Collaborative effort, exchange of information, and pooling of resources are essential for expediting the shift towards an environmentally sustainable and climate-change prepared future among countries. Sharing successful strategies, transferring technological knowledge, and providing financial aid to underdeveloped nations are vital ingredients in the global community's endeavors to tackle the pressing call for action.

Future of Global Warming Solutions

The significance of finding solutions for global warming cannot be overstated as it will have far-reaching implications for the well-being of our planet and future generations. In this pivotal moment in mankind's existence, it is glaringly obvious that prompt and revolutionary measures must be taken to confront the imminent and crucial issues brought about by the effects of global warming. Despite the seriousness of the situation, there are reasons for positivity and confidence because new ideas, advances in technology, and group endeavors are directing us towards a future that is eco-friendly and sustainable.

The potential for effective solutions to global warming appears to be particularly bright in the accelerated expansion of renewable energy sources. Significant progress has been made in the efficiency, affordability, and scalability of solar and wind power. Moving towards renewable energy not just lessens the impact of greenhouse gases but also lessens reliance on non-renewable resources, resulting in a boost in energy security and economic fortitude.

The forthcoming advancements in transportation offer enormous possibilities in promoting environmental solutions to combat global warming. The automotive industry is on the brink of a major transformation due to the swift progress of electric vehicles (EVs) and the widespread proliferation of charging infrastructure. As battery innovation advances, electric vehicles will become more cost-effective, presenting a practical and environmentally sound substitute for traditional automobiles. The merging of smart transportation systems, communal mobility offerings, and city planning that favors public transportation and eco-friendly modes such as biking and walking, can drastically diminish pollutants and optimize transportation infrastructures.

To combat the detrimental effects of climate change, the implementation of inventive agricultural practices and innovative land preservation methodologies is indispensable. By implementing sustainable practices like precision farming, agroforestry, and regenerative agriculture, it is possible to minimize the amount of greenhouse gases produced by farming, as well as improve soil health and increase carbon sequestration. Capturing carbon, preserving biodiversity, and safeguarding crucial ecosystem functions are reliant on the implementation of sustainable land management techniques like reforestation, afforestation, and preservation of natural habitats. To ensure the future of agriculture, it is imperative to adopt climate-conscious methods that prioritize sustainability and resilience, whilst also maintaining high levels of food production.

The integration of technology and data-driven solutions exhibits a significant potential to tackle challenges caused by global warming. By merging artificial intelligence, big data analytics, and IoT technology, users can make more intelligent decisions, maximize energy efficiency, effectively distribute resources, and accurately forecast climate changes. By leveraging the capabilities of these technologies, we can enhance our efforts in addressing the effects of climate change. This can empower us to react with increased precision and flexibility to mitigate and adapt to different climate scenarios.

The success of addressing global warming in the future is reliant on the cooperation and joint actions of various entities such as governments, corporations, communities, and individuals. It is crucial to have effective collaboration among nations driven by ambitious climate pacts to accomplish significant reductions in emissions worldwide. Governments at the national level are required to establish and apply measures that encourage sustainable behaviors, facilitate the advancement of clean technologies, and promote favorable conditions that attract investments in renewable energy. It is imperative for businesses to take on the responsibility of promoting innovation, adopting eco-friendly practices, and shifting towards business models with low carbon emissions. People have the power to make a positive impact by making mindful decisions about what they consume, minimizing unnecessary waste, and promoting sustainable ways of living.

Education and raising awareness play a critical role in shaping the way we resolve global warming issues. Educating people about climate change, its consequences, and possible remedies cultivates a sense of immediacy, accountability, and initiative among individuals. By including lessons about climate change in school courses, launching campaigns to raise public consciousness, and cultivating scientific understanding, we can develop a worldwide population confident in making informed choices and playing an active role in tackling climate problems.

The key to solving global warming lies in a comprehensive and interconnected strategy involving technological advancement, government backing, shifts in human behavior, and collaboration on a global scale. The way we produce and consume energy, handle our resources and land, and prioritize sustainability in every aspect of our lives must undergo a significant shift in order to move forward.

With the pressing nature of the climate emergency, it is necessary to take brave and resolute measures. It is crucial for governments to play an active role in implementing robust climate policies and objectives, as well as offering monetary rewards and fostering a conducive atmosphere for the adoption of renewable energy and sustainable practices. Simultaneously, it is necessary for businesses to adopt corporate sustainability practices, allocate resources towards eco-friendly technologies, and make environmental stewardship a fundamental principle of their operations.

It is important to involve both individuals and communities in an equal manner. Education and awareness initiatives must equip people with the knowledge to make informed decisions, embrace sustainable behaviors, and demand governmental action on climate change. Minor adjustments made by individuals, when magnified across communities, possess the ability to produce a substantial combined outcome.

In order to tackle global warming, it is imperative to work together on a global scale and foster international partnerships. The challenge of climate change goes beyond national boundaries, and coordinated actions must be taken to effectively confront it. Nations should fulfill their obligations outlined in global climate agreements, facilitate the exchange of information and technology, and furnish monetary and technical aid to developing countries.

The advancement and investigation play an essential role in promoting solutions to combat climate change. Working together, academic, industry and government organizations can drive innovation and create solutions that are both scalable and environmentally friendly.

It is crucial to keep in mind that addressing global warming is not only about reducing the effects of climate change but also about improving resilience and adjusting to the existing alterations. It is crucial to have a comprehensive approach that includes increasing our capacity to adjust to a fluctuating climate, protecting communities and ecosystems that are at risk, and advancing sustainable growth that prioritizes both current and future requirements.

The upcoming approaches to tackle global warming present both a difficulty and a chance for advancement. We can establish a more flourishing, fair, and wholesome world for ourselves and future generations by shifting our economies and lifestyles towards sustainability. We possess the expertise, the means, and the obligation to take action now.

References

Abrahamse & Steg, 2. (2013). Social influence approaches to encourage resource conservation: A meta-analysis. *Global Environmental Change, 23*(6), 1773-1785. doi:https://doi.org/10.1016/j.gloenvcha.2013.07.029

Adger et al., 2. (2003). Adaptation to climate change in the developing world. *SAGE Journals, 3*(3), 179-195. doi:10.1191/1464993403ps060oa

Ali, 2. (2021). Impact of climate change on food security and agricultural productivity: Evidence from Bangladesh. *Journal of Environmental Management, 279*(111768). doi:https://doi.org/10.1016/j.jenvman.2020.111768

Bamberg & Möser, 2. (2007). Twenty years after Hines, Hungerford, and Tomera: A new meta-analysis of psycho-social determinants of pro-environmental behaviour. *Journal of Environmental Psychology, 27*(1), 14-25. doi:DOI:10.1016/j.jenvp.2006.12.002

Barnett & O'Neill, 2. (2010). Maladaptation. Global Environmental Change. *Global Environmental Change, 20*(2), 211-213. doi:10.1016/j.gloenvcha.2009.11.004

Bélanger, J., & Pilling, D. (. (2019). *The State of the World's Biodiversity for Food and Agriculture.* Rome, Italy: FAO. doi:https://doi.org/10.4060/CA3129EN

Betsill & Bulkeley, 2. (2007). Looking back and thinking ahead: A decade of cities and climate change research. *Local Environment, 12*(5), 447-456. doi:10.1080/13549830701581550

Bruijnzeel et al., 2. (2011). *Tropical montane cloud forests: Science for conservation and management.* Cambridge University Press. Retrieved 2023

Bui et al., 2. (2018). Carbon capture and storage (CCS): the way forward. *Energy & Environmental Science, 11*(5), 1062-1176. doi:https://doi.org/10.1039/C7EE02342A

Bulkeley et al., 2. (2014). *Transnational Climate Change Governance.* Cambridge: Cambridge University Press. doi:doi:10.1017/CBO9781107706033

C2ES. (n.d.). *Climate Resilience Portal*. Retrieved from C2ES: https://www.c2es.org/content/climate-resilience-overview/

CDC, 2. (2022). *CDC's Building Resilience Against Climate Effects (BRACE) Framework*. Retrieved from Centers for Disease Control and Prevention: https://www.cdc.gov/climateandhealth/BRACE.htm

Chu & Majumdar, 2. (2012). Opportunities and challenges for a sustainable energy future. Nature. *Nature, 488*(7411), 294-303. doi:https://doi.org/10.1038/nature11475

Church & White, 2. (2011). Sea-Level Rise from the Late 19th to the Early 21st Century. *Surveys in Geophysics*, 585-602. doi:https://doi.org/10.1007/s10712-011-9119-1

Clayton et al., 2. (2015). Expanding the Role for Psychology in Addressing Environmental Challenges. *American Psychologist, 71*(3). doi:DOI:10.1037/a0039482

Dechezleprêtre et al., 2. (2010). What Drives the International Transfer of Climate Change Mitigation Technologies? Empirical Evidence from Patent Data. *Environmental and Resource Economics, 54*(2). doi:DOI:10.2139/ssrn.1558316

Deressa et al., 2. (2009). Determinants of farmers' choice of adaptation methods to climate change in the Nile Basin of Ethiopia. *Global Environmental Change, 19*(2), 248-255. doi:DOI:10.1016/j.gloenvcha.2009.01.002

Dolsak and Prakash, 2. (2018). *Understanding environmental policy change: A comparative analysis*. Routledge. Retrieved 2023

EDDY, J. A. (1976). The Maunder Minimum. *Science, 192*(4245), 1189-1202. doi: 10.1126/science.192.4245.1189

Ellen, M. (2021). *What is a circular economy?* Retrieved 2023, from (Ellen MacArthur Foundation: https://ellenmacarthurfoundation.org/topics/circular-economy-introduction/overview

Ellezelle et al., 2. (2022). Scaling Up of Nature-Based Solutions to Guide Climate Adaptation Planning: Evidence From Two Case Studies. *Frontiers in Sustainable Cities, 4*. doi:DOI={10.3389/frsc.2022.624046},

Fagnant & Kockelman, 2. (2015). The travel and environmental implications of shared autonomous vehicles, using agent-based model scenarios. *Transportation Research Part C: Emerging Technologies on Science Direct, 54*, 111-128. doi:https://doi.org/10.1016/j.trc.2015.02.001

Feldman et al., 2. (2014). The Mutual Reinforcement of Media Selectivity and Effects: Testing the Reinforcing Spirals Framework in the Context of Global Warming. *Journal of Communication, 64*(4), 590-611. doi:DOI:10.1111/jcom.12108

Folke et al., 2. (2005). Adaptive governance of social-ecological systems. *Annual Review of Environment and Resources, 30*, 441-473. doi:10.1146/annurev.energy.30.050504.144511

FUTURE, O. C. (n.d.). Climate Resilient SD: Movie in the Park Engagement Event. Retrieved from https://www.sandiego.gov/sites/default/files/crsd_comm unity_engagement_summary_final.pdf

Giles, J. e. (2021). Barriers to Implementing Climate Policies in Agriculture: A Case Study From Viet Nam. *Frontiers in Sustainable Food Systems, 5.* doi: https://doi.org/10.3389/fsufs.2021.439881

GLOBAL WARMING. (2018). Retrieved 2023, from Gale: https://www.gale.com/intl/databases-explored/social-issues/global-warming

Grossman et al., 2. (2019). Building resilience through community engagement in climate adaptation planning. *Journal of Environmental Planning and Management, 62*(5), 924-941. doi:10.1080/09640568.2018.1522286

Grubler et al., 2. (2018). A low energy demand scenario for meeting the 1.5 °C target and sustainable development goals without negative emission technologies. *Nature Energy, 3*(6). doi:DOI:10.1038/s41560-018-0172-6

Gupta et al., 2. (2010). The Adaptive Capacity Wheel: a method to assess the inherent characteristics of institutions to enable the adaptive capacity of society. *Environmental Science & Policy, 13*(6), 459-471. doi:https://doi.org/10.1016/j.envsci.2010.05.006

Helbling, M., & Meierrieks, D. (2022). Global warming and urbanization. *SpringerLink.*

Hussey, S. (n.d.). *Community Engagement.* Retrieved from GRANICUS: https://granicus.com/blog/community-engagement-steps-up-participation-in-climate-action/

IEA, 2. (2019). *Energy efficiency 2019.* Paris: IEA. Retrieved 2023, from https://www.iea.org/reports/energy-efficiency-2019

IMBRIE, J. I. (1980). Modeling the Climatic Response to Orbital Variations. *Science, 207*(4434), 943-953. doi:DOI: 10.1126/science.207.4434.943

IMF. (n.d.). *CLIMATE CHANGE | CLIMATE RESILIENCE.* Retrieved from International Monetary Fund: https://www.imf.org/en/Topics/climate-change/resilience-building

Ingrid et al., 2. (2022). What influences the implementation of natural climate solutions? A systematic map and review of the evidence. *Environmental Research Letters, 17*(1). doi:DOI:10.1088/1748-9326/ac4071

Ingrid Schulte et al., 2. (2021). What influences the implementation of natural climate solutions? A systematic map and review of the evidence. *Environmental Research Letters, 17*(1). doi:DOI 10.1088/1748-9326/ac4071

International Energy Agency, 2. (2020). *Net Zero by 2050: A Roadmap for the Global Energy Sector.* International Energy Agency (IEA). Retrieved 2023, from https://www.iea.org/reports/net-zero-by-2050

IRENA, 2. (2019). *Renewable power generation costs in 2018.* Retrieved 2023, from International Renewable Energy Agency: https://www.irena.org/-/media/Files/IRENA/Agency/Publication/2019/May/IRENA_Renewable-Power-Generations-Costs-in-2018.pdf

Jagers & Stripple, 2. (2021). Why market-based climate policy instruments succeed or fail: An overview of the dynamics of carbon pricing and emissions trading across different contexts. *Energy Research & Social Science, 102161*(80). doi:https://doi.org/10.1016/j.erss.2021.102161

JOSEPH E et al., 2. (2018). Natural climate solutions for the United States. *SCIENCE ADVANCES, 4*(11). doi:DOI: 10.1126/sciadv.aat1869

Kahan et al., 2. (2011). Cultural cognition of scientific consensus. *Journal of Risk Research, 14*(2), 147-174. doi:DOI:10.1080/13669877.2010.511246

Kahan et al., 2. (2012). The polarizing impact of science literacy and numeracy on perceived climate change risks. *Nature Climate Change, 2*(10), 732–735. doi:https://doi.org/10.1038/nclimate1547

Kim et al., 2. (2021). Barriers and Drivers for Mainstreaming Nature-Based Solutions for Flood Risks: The Case of South Korea. *Int J Disaster Risk Sci, 12*, 661–672. doi:https://doi.org/10.1007/s13753-021-00372-4

Kokei Otosi, 2. (2019). *Community Development*. Retrieved 2023, from Federal Reserve Bank of San Franscisco: https://www.frbsf.org/community-development/publications/community-development-investment-review/2019/october/promoting-equitable-climate-adaptation-through-community-engagement/

Le et al., 2. (2020). Understanding the impacts of climate change on African landscapes: Progress and challenges. *Earth-Science Reviews, 210*(103276). doi:https://doi.org/10.1016/j.earscirev.2020.103276

Leiserowitz et al, .. 2. (2006). Climate change risk perception and policy preferences: The role of affect, imagery, and values. *Climatic Change, 77*(1-2), 45–72. doi:https://doi.org/10.1007/s10584-006-9059-9

Litman, 2. (2020). *Evaluating transportation equity*. Retrieved 2023, from Victoria Transport Policy Institute: https://www.vtpi.org/equity.pdf

MacArthur, E. (2017). *A New Textiles Economy: Redesigning fashion's future*. Retrieved 2023, from Ellen MacArthur Foundation: https://ellenmacarthurfoundation.org/a-new-textiles-economy

Makau et al., 2. (2020). Ecosystem-based adaptation practices: The role of indigenous trees and shrubs in mitigating climate change in Kenya. *17*(3), 856. doi:10.3390/ijerph17030856

Masson-Delmotte et al., 2. (2018). *Global Warming of 1.5°C.* Cambridge, UK and New York, NY, USA: Cambridge University Press. doi:doi:10.1017/9781009157940

McCright & Dunlap, 2. (2011). The Politicization of Climate Change and Polarization in the American Public's Views of Global Warming, 2001–2010. *The Sociological Quarterly, 52*(2), 155-194. doi:https://doi.org/10.1111/j.1533-8525.2011.01198.x

McCright & Dunlap, 2. (2011). The Politicization Of Climate Change And Polarization In The American Public's Views Of Global Warming, 2001-2010. *The Sociological Quarterly, 52*(2), 155 - 194. doi:DOI:10.1111/j.1533-8525.2011.01198.x

Milesi et al., 2. (2005). Mapping and Modeling the Biogeochemical Cycling of Turf Grasses in the United States. *Environmental Management,* 426–438. doi:https://doi.org/10.1007/s00267-004-0316-2

Milfont & Duckitt, 2. (2010). The Environmental Attitudes Inventory: A valid and reliable measure to assess the structure of environmental attitudes. *Journal of Environmental Psychology, 30*(1), 80-94. doi:DOI:10.1016/j.jenvp.2009.09.001

Milfont & Sibley, 2. (2014). The big five personality traits and environmental engagement: Associations at the individual and societal level. *Journal of Environmental Psychology, 32*(2), 187–195. doi:DOI:10.1016/j.jenvp.2011.12.006

Nisbet & Myers, 2. (2007). Twenty Years of Public Opinion about Global Warming. *Public Opinion Quarterly, 71*(3), 444-470. doi:doi:10.1093/poq/nfm031

Nolan et al., 2. (2008). Normative social influence is underdetected. *Personality and Social Psychology Bulletin, 34*(7), 913–923. doi: https://doi.org/10.1177/0146167208316691

Nordborg & Karlsson, 2. (2019). A framework for understanding the potential of renewable energy sources in industrial applications. *Energy Policy on Science Direct*, 319-328. doi:https://doi.org/10.1016/j.enpol.2018.12.044

NUNEZ, C. (2019, JANUARY 23). *What is global warming, explained*. Retrieved 2023, from National Geographic: https://www.nationalgeographic.com/environment/articl e/global-warming-overview

Parmesan, C. (. (2006). Ecological and evolutionary responses to recent climate change. *Annual Review of Ecology, Evolution, and Systematics, 37,* 637-669. doi:https://doi.org/10.1126/science.287.5459.1770

Patterson et al., 2. (2017). Exploring the governance and politics of transformations towards sustainability. *Environmental Innovation and Societal Transitions, 24,* 1-16. doi:https://doi.org/10.1016/j.eist.2016.09.001

Peters and Hertwich, 2. (2008). Post-Kyoto greenhouse gas inventories: production versus consumption. *Climate Change,* 51–66 . doi:https://doi.org/10.1007/s10584-007-9280-1

Ranganathan et al., 2. (2016). *Installment 11 of "Creating a Sustainable Food Future" SHIFTING DIETS FOR A.* Retrieved 2023, from World Resources Institute: https://wriorg.s3.amazonaws.com/s3fs-public/Shifting_Diets_for_a_Sustainable_Food_Future_ 1.pdf

Reed et al., 2. (2010). What is social learning? *Ecology and Society, 15*(4), 1-14. doi: 10.5751/ES-03564-150401

Ribeiro et al., 2. (2017). The Brazilian Atlantic Forest: How much is left, and how is the remaining forest distributed? *Biological Conservation, 142*(6), 1141-1153. doi:10.1016/j.biocon.2009.02.021

Rosenzweig et al., 2. (2008). Attributing physical and biological impacts to anthropogenic climate change. *Nature,* 353-357. doi:https://doi.org/10.1038/nature06937

Rosenzweig et al., 2. (2008). Attributing physical and biological impacts to anthropogenic climate change. *Nature, 453*(7193), 353-357. doi: https://doi.org/10.1038/nature06937

Sala et al., 2. (2000). Global biodiversity scenarios for the year 2100. *Science, 287*(5459), 1770-1774. doi:https://doi.org/10.1126/science.287.5459.1770

Sala et al., 2. (2000). Global biodiversity scenarios for the year 2100. *Science, 287*(5459), 1770-1774. doi:https://doi.org/10.1126/science.287.5459.1770

Samsatli et al., 2. (2018). Design and operational optimisation of hydrogen supply chains: A review and a proposed approach. *Science Direct,* 158-187. doi:https://doi.org/10.1016/j.compchemeng.2018.02.024

Scherer et al., 2. (2014). *Ecosystem-based approaches to climate change adaptation – concepts, potentials and limitations.* Wiley-Blackwell. Retrieved 2023

Schlosberg & Collins, 2. (2014). From environmental to climate justice: Climate change and the discourse of environmental justice. *Wiley Interdisciplinary Reviews: Climate Change.* doi:DOI:10.1002/wcc.275

Schultz et al., 2. (2005). Implicit connections with nature. *Journal of Environmental Psychology, 24*(1), 31–42. doi: https://doi.org/10.1016/S0272-4944(03)00022-7

Sherry Spiers et al. (n.d.). Adaptation Planning Stakeholder. Retrieved from https://floridadep.gov/sites/default/files/CRI_Adaptation _Planning_Stakeholder_Outreach_and_Engagement%3 B_2017.pdf

Skocpol & Williamson, 2. (2012). *The Tea Party and the remaking of Republican conservatism.* Oxford University Press. Retrieved 2023

Smit & Wandel, 2. (2006). Adaptation, adaptive capacity and vulnerability. Global Environmental Change. *Global Environmental Change, 16*(3), 282-292. doi:10.1016/j.gloenvcha.2006.03.008

Sovacool et al., 2. (2020). Culture and low-carbon energy transitions. *Nature Sustainability, 3*(9), 1-9. doi:doi = {10.1038/s41893-020-0519-4}

Spence et al., 2. (2012). The Psychological Distance of Climate Change. *Risk Analysis, 32*(6), 957-972. doi: https://doi.org/10.1111/j.1539-6924.2011.01695.x

Stavins, 2. (2019). The Future of US Carbon Pricing Policy. *Journal of Economic Perspectives, 33*(4), 3-26. doi:https://doi.org/10.1257/jep.33.4.3

Steffen et al., 2. (2015). The Trajectory of the Anthropocene: The Great Acceleration. *The Anthropocene Review*. doi:DOI:10.1177/2053019614564785

Stern, 2. (2000). New Environmental Theories: Toward a Coherent Theory of Environmentally Significant Behavior. *Journal of Social Issues, 56*(3), 407-424. doi: https://doi.org/10.1111/0022-4537.00175

STOTHERS, R. B. (1984). The Great Tambora Eruption in 1815 and Its Aftermath. *Science, 224*(4654), 1191-1198. doi: 10.1126/science.224.4654.1191

Susanne Moser, 2. (2015). Community engagement on adaptation: Meeting a growing capacity need. *Urban Climate, 14*. doi:http://dx.doi.org/10.1016/j.uclim.2015.06.006

The World Bank, 2. (2020). *The Adaptation Principles: 6 Ways to Build Resilience to Climate Change*. Retrieved from Worldbank: https://www.worldbank.org/en/news/feature/2020/11/17/the-adaptation-principles-6-ways-to-build-resilience-to-climate-change

World101). (n.d.). *How Do Governments Combat Climate Change?* Retrieved from world101.cfr.org: https://world101.cfr.org/global-era-issues/climate-change/how-do-governments-combat-climate-change